D0017638

TRAINSPOTTING

TRAINSPOTTING

John Hodge

New York

Copyright © 1996, John Hodge
Introduction © John Hodge, 1996
Afterword © Irvine Welsh and Kevin Macdonald, 1996
Photographs by Liam Longman

Previously published in Great Britain by Faber and Faber

All rights reserved. No part of this book may be used or repro-
duced in any manner whatsoever without written permission
of the Publisher. Printed in the United States of America. For
information address Hyperion, 114 Fifth Avenue, New York,
NY 10011.

ISBN 0-7868-8221-2

First American Edition

10 9 8 7 6 5 4 3 2 1

CONTENTS

INTRODUCTION

I began writing *Shallow Grave* in the spring of 1991. If I had known then what I know now about the coalition of fortune and favour that must occur before a script becomes a film, I would not have bothered. I knew nothing and no one. I naïvely assumed that all I had to do was write what I liked and all the necessary people would fall into place. They would take the script from my hands and turn it into the film I wanted to see. That this is more or less exactly what happened is a tribute to the beneficial effects of ignorance.

I had this idea about three people in a flat and a stranger and a bag of money and that seemed to me like a film, so I began writing. With a view to an end-of-career auction, the first draft of *Shallow Grave* was hand-written on table napkins, backs of envelopes, etc. I showed it to my sister who introduced me to a guy called Andrew Macdonald who said that he was a 'producer'. This was a lie. He told me that he had worked in Hollywood as a script editor. This was a lie. He told me that he had met Bridget Fonda; that he knew Bridget Fonda well, and implied, more or less, that he had enjoyed a tabloid celebrity-style on-off relationship with Bridget Fonda for several years and that it was only a matter of time before I saw her on the cover of *Hello!* magazine under the headline 'Coping without Andrew: Bridget Fonda's Inner Strength'. He assured me that she would star in our film, along with Ray Liotta and Bill Murray (the two male leads I had in mind). Need I say that this was all one big lie?

I soon discovered the true nature of Macdonald's work 'in television' when I visited the set of *Taggart* and was witness to the spectacle of Bridget Fonda's on-off lover replenishing the store of Andrex in the extras' toilets and then spooning tuna to the leading lady's cat.

But Macdonald and I established a healthy working relationship. I would write a new draft of the script which he would then read and then return with a tactful critique like, 'The second half isn't up to much.' Holding back the tears, I would review the section in question and, to my regular irritation, find myself in agreement. I then indulged in orgies of bloodletting, striking out subplots, characters, and locations, and a couple of months later we would do it all over again.

After about a year and half of this we found ourselves in the offices of Channel Four facing two responsible adults who liked the script but wanted to know just who did we think we were. I would have immediately confessed to our status as bona fide no-hopers but Macdonald intervened and revealed why he is a producer and I am not. I sat in awed silence while he calmly described his background in 'film' and 'television': the formative experiences at Pinewood and Shepperton (back in the days when there was British film industry, of course), the Hollywood years, the loss of faith in the studio system, the return to small-scale, low-budget short film-making, the directorial dabbling, and the limitless commercial and artistic vision. The only thing he missed out was the on-off love affair with Bridget Fonda. It was a marvellous performance. We were instructed to return with a new draft, a budget, and a director.

So while I sweated out another new draft, Macdonald spent the next two months having lunch, which is apparently the accepted method of finding a director.

Danny Boyle was not what I expected. Where were the jodhpurs, the beret, and the megaphone? In conversation he came across as a man of sensitivity and endless patience but with a thuggish streak and a certain low, animal cunning: in short, a man who could work with actors. Any doubts I might have harboured were blown away on our first return to the responsible adults, when Boyle answered the question of how he would direct the film by saying that it would be 'witty, but not expressionist'. I have often pondered on the meaning of this phrase, wondering whether or not it would be altered by rearranging the words.

A few more rewrites were undertaken as the summer drifted by and filming drew ever nearer. My involvement gradually faded out until I reached the role of constitutional monarch, consulted on everything on the understanding that the answer would be 'yes'. This is the writer's lot: anyone who doesn't like it should learn either to lie or to work with actors. I began to plan my retirement.

PART TWO: THE FINAL DAYS

In February 1994, a few months after the shooting of *Shallow Grave* had finished, Macdonald visited me in my south-coast rest home where he gave me a copy of *Trainspotting* by Irvine Welsh and suggested I read it with a view to screen adaptation. I took the book, read it, and, suitably stunned, I handed it back.

Trainspotting is an incredible book: its characters, language, narratives, and tone of aggressive entertainment were like nothing I had seen before.

I explained to Macdonald why *Trainspotting* would never make a film.

1) It is a collection of loosely related short stories about several different characters. Only towards the end does it take on a continuous narrative form.

2) The characters, each with a distinctive voice, are defined by internal monologue as much as anything, and the language is uncompromisingly specific to a time and place.

In addition, I pointed out that I had retired from screenwriting.

But Macdonald persisted, implying in a strictly off the record, noncommittal way that my fee might be larger this time. Furthermore, he observed, with perhaps half a century of life ahead of me this charming rest home with its view across to France on a clear day could soon be beyond my means. Thus enslaved again in the degrading business of film, I reread *Trainspotting*. I enjoyed it even more, noticing depth and humanity that I had missed the first time around, having been dazzled then by the language and the horror. But still I didn't see it as a film. Boyle and Macdonald, not being screenwriters (unlike me with my one credit to prove it), were not put off by my protest about the practical difficulties. Their confidence was touching and their suggestions were many even if, at times, they fell short of actually being helpful. Months went by, then some more months, and still they nagged on. I agreed to a two-week brain-storming session to hammer it out once and for all, expecting that either this would be the end of it, or that late at night over takeaway pizza and cold coffee (American cop show fantasy time again) one of us would stand back from the shaving mirror and say: 'I've got it.'

Unfortunately this was not the end of it and there was no takeaway pizza. I went home at five o'clock every day after several hours of discussion on the relative merits of 'sex with the deceased brother's pregnant widow' versus 'fishing through strangers' excrement for the lost morphine suppositories'. Tough one, that.

At the end of this fortnight, Boyle and Macdonald, now quite exhausted by all that thinking but happy that they had given their all to the scripting process, retired to lie in darkened rooms and await the soft plop of script through letterbox.

I read the book again and started writing. My intention was to produce a screenplay which would seem to have, approximately, a beginning, a middle, and an end, would last ninety minutes, and would convey at least some of the spirit and content of the book. This involved amalgamating various characters, transferring incident and dialogue from one character to another, building some scenes around minor details from the book and making up a few things altogether.

If I missed out your favourite bits, well I'm sorry but I missed out some of my own as well. 'Memories of Matty', for example, is probably my favourite chapter: it has enough material for a whole film in itself, but too much to fit into a single scene in this version. All that survives from it is Spud's attention to Australian pop culture after Tommy's funeral, but even that moment is left unexplained in the forward rush of screen time. For a more complete understanding of that scene and all others, please refer to the book.

My own contributions to the script make up a small proportion of it and are not crucial. I am proud, however, to have found a fitting monument at last for Archie Gemmill's goal against Holland in 1978. A whole nation of gullible males was moved by feelings of disappointment, betrayal, and ecstasy during that summer. Seventeen years later it seemed an ideal emotional cocktail for Mark Renton.

It should be stated that throughout this process Irvine Welsh was a saintly model of non-intervention while a complete stranger took liberties with his text. I cannot imagine many authors being so relaxed, especially when the work in question has been recognized as a classic and has found such devotion in the minds of its readers.

I would like to thank the people who helped to construct both these scripts and specifically the following who have all contributed criticism at one time or another: Grace Hodge, Andrew Macdonald, Danny Boyle, David Aukin, Jack Lechner, Allon Reich, Allan Shiach, Chris Young, Marc Berlin, and Walter Donohue. And finally, thank you, Mother and Father, for all the encouragement and support that you have given.

John Hodge
November 1995

Andrew Macdonald, John Hodge and Danny Boyle on location for *Trainspotting*.

TRAINSPOTTING

EXT. STREET. DAY

Legs run along the pavement. They are Mark Renton's.

Just ahead of him is Spud. They are both belting along.

As they travel, various objects (pens, tapes, CDs, toiletries, ties, sunglasses, etc.) either fall or are discarded from inside their jackets.

They are pursued by two hard-looking Store Detectives in identical uniforms. The men are fast, but Renton and Spud maintain their lead.

RENTON
(*voice-over*)

Choose life. Choose a job. Choose a career. Choose a family. Choose a fucking big television, choose washing machines, cars, compact disc players and electrical tin openers.

Suddenly, as Renton crosses a road, a car skids to a halt, inches from him.

In a moment of detachment he stops and looks at the shocked driver, then at Spud, who has continued running, then at the Two Men, who are now closing on him.

He smiles.

INT. SWANNEY'S FLAT ROOM. DAY

In a bare, dingy room, Renton lies on the floor, alone, motionless and drugged.

RENTON
(*voice-over*)

Choose good health, low cholesterol and dental insurance. Choose fixed-interest mortgage repayments. Choose a starter home. Choose your friends.

EXT. FOOTBALL PITCH. NIGHT

On a floodlit five-a-side pitch, Renton and his friends are taking on another team at football.

The opposition all wear an identical strip (Arsenal), whereas Renton and his friends wear an odd assortment of gear.

Three girls – Lizzy, Gail and Allison and Baby – stand by the side, watching.

The boys are outclassed by the team with the strip but play much dirtier.

As each performs a characteristic bit of play, the play freezes and their name is visible, printed or written on some item of clothing (T-shirt, baseball cap, shorts, trainers). In Begbie's case, his name appears as a tattoo on his arm.

Sick Boy commits a sneaky foul and indignantly denies it.

Begbie commits an obvious foul and makes no effort to deny it.

Spud, in goal, lets the ball in between his legs.

Tommy kicks the ball as hard as he can.

Renton's litany continues over the action:

RENTON
(voice-over)

Choose leisurewear and matching luggage. Choose a three-piece suite on hire purchase in a range of fucking fabrics. Choose DIY and wondering who the fuck you are on a Sunday morning. Choose sitting on that couch watching mind-numbing, spirit-crushing game shows, stuffing fucking junk food into your mouth. Choose rotting away at the end of it all, pishing your last in a miserable home, nothing more than an embarrassment to the selfish, fucked-up brats you have spawned to replace yourself. Choose your future. Choose life.

> *Renton is hit straight in the face by the ball. He lies back on the astroturf. Voice-over continues.*

But why would I want to do a thing like that?

4

INT. SWANNEY'S FLAT. DAY

Renton lies on the floor.

Swanney, Allison and Baby, Sick Boy and Spud are shooting up or preparing to shoot up. Sick Boy is talking to Allison as he taps up a vein on her arm.

RENTON
(*voice-over*)

I chose not to choose life: I chose something else. And the reasons? There are no reasons. Who needs reasons when you've got heroin?

SICK BOY

Goldfinger's better than *Dr No*. Both of them are a lot better than *Diamonds are Forever*, a judgement reflected in its relative poor showing at the box office, in which field, of course, *Thunderball* was a notable success.

RENTON
(*voice-over*)

People think it's all about misery and desperation and death and all that shite, which is not to be ignored, but what they forget –

Spud is shooting up.

is the pleasure of it. Otherwise we wouldn't do it. After all, we're not fucking stupid. At least, we're not that fucking stupid. Take the best orgasm you ever had, multiply it by a thousand and you're still nowhere near it. When you're on junk you have only one worry: scoring. When you're off it you are suddenly obliged to worry about all sorts of other shite. Got no money: can't get pished. Got money: drinking too much. Can't get a bird: no chance of a ride. Got a bird: too much hassle. You have to worry about bills, about food, about some football team that never fucking wins, about human relationships and all the things that really don't matter when you've got a sincere and truthful junk habit.

SICK BOY

I would say, in those days, he was a muscular actor, in every sense, with all the presence of someone like Cooper or Lancaster, but

5

combined with a sly wit to make him a formidable romantic lead, closer in that respect to Cary Grant.

                    RENTON
                  (voice-over)
The only drawback, or at least the principal drawback, is that you have to endure all manner of cunts telling you that –

INT. PUB I. NIGHT

Begbie, smoking and drinking, speaks to camera.

                    BEGBIE
No way would I poison my body with that shite, all they fucking chemicals, no fucking way.

INT. PUB I. NIGHT

Tommy sits beside Lizzy. He speaks to camera.

                    TOMMY
It's a waste of your life, Rents, poisoning your body with that shite.

INT. RENTON FAMILY HOME, LIVING ROOM. NIGHT

Renton's father and mother sit at the table eating.

Renton is seated but not eating.

                    FATHER
Every chance you've ever had, you've blown it, stuffing your veins with that filth.

*[INT. ELECTRICAL RETAILERS. DAY

Gav wears the corporate jacket.

                    GAV
Get off that stuff, Rents, and get a job. It's not as bad as it looks. While you're here, you don't fancy buying a cooker, do you?]

*Cut from completed film.

INT. SWANNEY'S FLAT. DAY

Sick Boy and Spud lie drugged up. Allison and Baby wait while Swanney cooks up.

Renton is standing up.

> **RENTON**
> (*voice-over*)
> From time to time, even I have uttered the magic words.

> **SWANNEY**
> Are you serious?

> **RENTON**
> Yeah. No more. I'm finished with that shite.

> **SWANNEY**
> Well, it's up to you.

> **RENTON**
> I'm going to get it right this time. Going to get it set up and get off it for good.

> **SWANNEY**
> Sure, sure. I've heard it before.

> **RENTON**
> The Sick Boy method.

They both look at Sick Boy.

> **SWANNEY**
> Yeah, well, it surely worked for him.

> **RENTON**
> He's always been lacking in moral fibre.

> **SWANNEY**
> He knows a lot about Sean Connery.

> **RENTON**
> That's hardly a substitute.

> **SWANNEY**
> You'll need one more hit.

RENTON
No, I don't think so.

SWANNEY

To see you through the night that lies ahead.

Freeze frame on Swanney.

RENTON
(voice-over)

We called him the mother superior on account of the length of his habit. He knew all about it. On it, off it, he knew it all. Of course I'd have another shot: after all, I had work to do.

INT. RENTON'S FLAT ROOM. DAY

The door opens and Renton enters carrying shopping bags. He empties them on to a mattress beside three buckets and a television.

RENTON
(voice-over)

Relinquishing junk. Stage One: preparation. For this you will need: one room which you will not leave; one mattress; tomato soup, ten tins of; mushroom soup, eight tins of, for consumption cold; ice cream, vanilla, one large tub of; Magnesia, Milk of, one bottle; paracetamol; mouth wash; vitamins; mineral water; Lucozade; pornography; one bucket for urine, one for faeces, and one for vomitus; one television; and one bottle of Valium, which I have already procured, from my mother, who is, in her own domestic and socially aceptable way, also a drug addict.

Renton swallows several Valium tablets. Voice-over continues.

And now I'm ready. All I need is a final hit to soothe the pain while the Valium takes effect.

*[INT. SWANNEY'S FLAT. DAY

Swanney, Sick Boy, Spud and Allison and Baby all lie inert while the telephone rings.]

*Cut from completed film.

INT. CALL BOX. DAY

Renton curses as he slams down the receiver. He dials again.

RENTON
Mikey. It's Mark Renton. Can you help me out?

INT. MIKEY'S FLAT. DAY

Renton holds two opium suppositories in the palm of his hand.

RENTON
(*voice-over*)
This was typical of Mikey Forrester.
(*on screen*)
What the fuck are these?
(*voice-over*)
Under the normal run of things I would have had nothing to do
with the cunt, but this was not the normal run of things.

MIKEY
Opium suppositories. Ideal for your purpose. Slow release, like.
Bring you down gradually. Custom fucking designed for your
needs.

RENTON
I want a fucking hit.

MIKEY
That's all I've got: take it or leave it.

*Renton sticks his hand down the back of his trousers and sticks the
suppositories into his rectum.*

Feel better now?

RENTON
For all the good they've done me I might as well have stuck them
up my arse.

He smiles.

11

EXT. STREET. DAY

> RENTON
> (*voice-over*)

Heroin makes you constipated. The heroin from my last hit is fading away and the suppositories have yet to melt. I am no longer constipated.

He looks around the local amenities. He is in discomfort, clutching his abdomen and falling to his knees.

He notices a betting shop.

INT. BETTING SHOP. DAY

Renton walks through the crowded, smoky betting shop towards a door market 'toilet' with a bit of card.

> RENTON
> (*voice-over*)

I fantasize about a massive pristine convenience.

He stumbles through.

> (*voice-over*)

Brilliant gold taps, virginal white marble, a seat carved from ebony, a cistern full of Chanel No. 5, and a flunky handing me pieces of raw silk toilet roll. But under the circumstances I'll settle for anywhere.

INT. HORRIBLE TOILET. DAY

This is the most horrible toilet in Britain.

Alone, Renton makes his way through the horrors to a cubicle.

INT. HORRIBLE TOILET CUBICLE. DAY

Renton locks the door.

He looks into the bowl and winces with disgust, even in his state.

He pulls the chain. The chain comes off.

He drops his trousers, sits on the bowl and closes his eyes.

*[MONTAGE

A lorry on a buliding site dumps a load of bricks, B52s shed their load on Vietnam, the Blue Peter *elephant, etc.*]

INT. CUBICLE. DAY

Renton has his eyes closed. They snap open.

He looks down between his legs.

He drops to his knees in front of the bowl and rolls his sleeve up.

With no more hesitation he plunges his arm into the bowl and trawls for the suppositories.

It seems to take ages. He cannot find them. He sticks his arm further and further into the toilet, moving his whole body closer. He strains to find it.

His head is over the bowl now. Gradually he reaches still further until his head is lowered into the bowl, followed by his neck, torso, other arm, and finally his legs, all disappearing.

The cubicle is empty.

INT. UNDER WATER. DAY

Renton, dressed as before, swims through murky depths until he reaches the bottom, where he picks up the suppositories, which glow like luminous pearls, before heading up towards the surface again.

INT. HORRIBLE TOILET CUBICLE. DAY

The toilet is empty.

Suddenly Renton appears through the bowl, then his arms as he lifts himself out. Still clasping his two suppositories, he walks out of the toilet.

INT. RENTON'S ROOM. DAY

The mattress, buckets and supplies are laid out as before.

The door opens and Renton enters, still soaking and dripping.

*Cut from completed film.

13

The suppositories are in his hand. He holds them up, and they twinkle in the light.

                    RENTON
Now. Now I'm ready.

INT. RENTON'S ROOM. DAY

The cans of soup, the bottle of water and the carton of ice cream are empty, the bottles of pills spilt, the magazines well thumbed.

★[SICK BOY
You Only Live Twice?

                    RENTON
Nineteen-sixty-seven.

                    SICK BOY
Running time?

                    RENTON
One hundred and sixteen minutes.

                    SICK BOY
Director?

                    RENTON
Lewis Gilbert.

                    SICK BOY
Screenwriter?

                    RENTON
Eh – Ian Fleming?

                    SICK BOY
Fuck off! He never wrote any of them.

                    RENTON
OK, so who was it, then?

                    SICK BOY
You can look it up.

*Cut from completed film.

14

Sick Boy throws across a worn copy of a film guide. Renton cannot be bothered to pick it up.

How are you feeling since you came off the skag? For myself, I'm bored.

RENTON

Who wrote it?

SICK BOY

But you're looking better, it has to be said. Healthier. Radiant even.

RENTON

You don't know, do you?

SICK BOY

And I wondered if you'd care to go to the park tomorrow.

RENTON

The park?

SICK BOY

Tomorrow afternoon. Usual set-up.

RENTON

Who wrote it?

SICK BOY

Roald Dahl.

RENTON

Roald Dahl. Fuck me.]

EXT. PARK. DAY

Typical weather, neither good nor bad. The park is nondescript arid green with a few bushes. This is not Kew Gardens. Renton and Sick Boy appear, dressed as before but for the addition of cheap sunglasses.

Renton is carrying a battered old cassette player and a carry-out in a plastic bag.

Sick Boy is carrying a small, tatty suitcase from Oxfam.

They scan the horizon and give each other the nod. They walk towards the bushes.

RENTON
(*voice-over*)

The downside of coming off junk was that I knew I would need to mix with my friends again in a state of full consciousness. It was awful: they reminded me so much of myself I could hardly bear to look at them. Take Sick Boy, for instance, he came off junk at the same time as me, not because he wanted to, you understand, but just to annoy me, just to show me how easily he could do it, thereby downgrading my own struggle. Sneaky fucker, don't you think? And when all I wanted to do was lie alone and feel sorry for myself, he insisted on telling me once again about his unifying theory of life.

EXT. PARK. DAY

Seen through the telescopic sight of an air rifle that wanders over various potential targets (children, pensioners, couples, gardeners, etc.).

SICK BOY
It's certainly a phenomenon in all walks of life.

RENTON
What do you mean?

SICK BOY
Well, at one time, you've got it, and then you lose it, and it's gone for ever. All walks of life: George Best, for example, had it and lost it, or David Bowie, or Lou Reed –

RENTON
Some of his solo stuff's not bad.

SICK BOY
No, it's not bad, but it's not great either, is it? And in your heart you kind of know that although it sounds all right, it's actually just shite.

RENTON
So who else?

SICK BOY
Charlie Nicholas, David Niven, Malcolm McLaren, Elvis Presley –

RENTON

OK, OK, so what's the point you're trying to make?

EXT. PARK. DAY

Sick Boy rests the gun down.

SICK BOY

All I'm trying to do is help you understand that *The Name of the Rose* is merely a blip on an otherwise uninterrupted downward trajectory.

RENTON

What about *The Untouchables*?

SICK BOY

I don't rate that at all.

RENTON

Despite the Academy award?

SICK BOY

That means fuck all. The sympathy vote.

RENTON

Right. So we all get old and then we can't hack it any more. Is that
it?

SICK BOY

Yeah.

RENTON

That's your theory?

SICK BOY

Yeah. Beautifully fucking illustrated.

RENTON

Give me the gun.

EXT. PARK. DAY

*Through the sight again. This time a Skinhead and his muscle-bound
dog are in view.*

Sick Boy and Renton talk like Sean Connery.

SICK BOY

Do you see the beast? Have you got it in your sights?

RENTON

Clear enough, Moneypenny. This should present no significant
problem.

*The gun fires and the dog yelps, jumps up and bites its owner (the
Skinhead).*

SICK BOY

For a vegetarian, Rents, you're a fucking evil shot.

EXT. PARK. DAY

Renton loads up again.

RENTON
(*voice-over*)

Without heroin, I attempted to lead a useful and fulfilling life as a
good citizen.

INT. CAFÉ. DAY

Two milkshakes clink together.

Renton and Spud are seated at a booth, dressed in their own fashion for job interviews.

> RENTON

Good luck, Spud.

> SPUD

Cheers.

> RENTON

Now remember –

> SPUD

Yeah.

> RENTON

If they think you're not trying, you're in trouble. First hint of that, they'll be on to the DSS, 'This cunt's no trying' and your Giro is fucking finished, right?

> SPUD

Right.

RENTON

But try too hard –

SPUD

And you might get the fucking job.

RENTON

Exactly.

SPUD

Nightmare.

RENTON

It's a tightrope, Spud, a fucking tightrope.

SPUD

My problem is that I tend to clam up. I go dumb and I can't answer any questions at all. Nerves on the big occasion, like a footballer.

RENTON

Try this.

Renton unfolds silver foil to reveal some amphetamine. Spud dips in a finger and takes a dab. He nods in appreciation as he tastes it. Renton leaves the packet in Spud's hand.

SPUD

A little dab of speed is just the ticket.

*[INT. INTERVIEW OFFICE. DAY

A Woman and Two Men (1 and 2) are interviewing Renton. His job application form is on the desk in front of them.

MAN I

Well, Mr Renton, I see that you attended the Royal Edinburgh College.

RENTON

Indeed, yes, those halcyon days.

*Cut from completed film.

MAN I

One of Edinburgh's finest schools.

RENTON

Oh, yes, indeed. I look back on my time there with great fondness
and affection. The debating society, the first eleven, the soft knock
of willow on leather –

MAN I

I'm an old boy myself, you know?

RENTON

Oh, really?

MAN I

Do you recall the school motto?

RENTON

Of course, the motto, the motto –

MAN I

Strive, hope, believe and conquer.

RENTON

Exactly. Those very words have been my guiding light in what is,
after all, a dark and often hostile world.

Renton looks pious under scrutiny.

MAN 2

Mr Renton –

RENTON

Yes.

MAN 2

You seem eminently suited to this post but I wonder if you could
explain the gaps in your employment record?

RENTON

Yes, I can. The truth – well, the truth is that I've had a long-
standing problem with heroin addiction. I've been known to sniff
it, smoke it, swallow it, stick it up my arse and inject it into my
veins. I've been trying to combat this addiction, but unless you
count social security scams and shoplifting, I haven't had a regular

21

job in years. I feel it's important to mention this.

There is silence.

A paper clip crashes to the floor.]

INT. OFFICE. DAY

The same office. The same team are interviewing Spud.

SPUD

No, actually I went to Craignewton but I was worried that you
wouldn't have heard of it so I put the Royal Edinburgh College
instead, because they're both schools, right, and we're all in this
together, and I wanted to put across the general idea rather than
the details, yeah? People get all hung up on details, but what's the
point? Like which school? Does it matter? Why? When? Where?
Or how many O grades did I get? Could be six, could be one, but
that's not important. What's important is that I am, right? That I
am.

MAN 1

Mr Murphy, do you mean that you lied on your application?

SPUD

Only to get my foot in the door. Showing initiative, right?

MAN 1

You were referred here by the Department of Employment.
There's no need for you to get your 'foot in the door', as you put
it.

SPUD

Hey. Right. No problem. Whatever you say, man. You're the
man, the governor, the dude in the chair, like. I'm merely here.
But obviously I am. Here, that is. I hope I'm not talking too
much. I don't usually. I think it's all important though, isn't it?

MAN 2

Mr Murphy, what attracts you to the leisure industry?

SPUD

In a word, pleasure. My pleasure in other people's leisure.

*[**WOMAN**
What do you see as your main strengths?

SPUD
I love people. All people. Even people that no one else loves, I think they're OK, you know. Like Beggars.

WOMAN
Homeless people?

SPUD
No, not homeless people. Beggars, Francis Begbie – one of my mates. I wouldn't say my best mate, I mean, sometimes the boy goes over the score, like one time when we – me and him – were having a laugh and all of a sudden he's fucking gubbed me in the face, right –]

WOMAN
Mr Murphy, *[leaving your friend aside,] do you see yourself as having any weaknesses?

SPUD
I have to admit it: I'm a perfectionist. For me, it's the best or nothing at all. If things go badly, I can't be bothered, but I have a good feeling about this interview. Seems to me like it's gone pretty well. We've touched on a lot of subjects, a lot of things to think about, for all of us.

MAN I
Thank you, Mr Murphy. We'll let you know.

SPUD
The pleasure was mine. Best interview I've ever been to. Thanks.

Spud crosses the room to shake everyone by the hand and kiss them.

RENTON
(*voice-over*)
Spud had done well. I was proud of him. He fucked up good and proper.

*Cut from completed film.

*[INT. PUB I. DAY

Renton and Spud meet up after the interviews.

SPUD

A little too well, if anything, a little too well, that's my only fear, compadre.

RENTON

Another dab?

SPUD

Would not say no, would not say no.

INT. OFFICE. DAY

The Woman and Two Men sit in silence.]

INT. PUB 2. NIGHT

It is Saturday night in a busy, city-centre pub on two levels. On a large upper balcony, overlooking the bar and floor downstairs, sit Spud, Gail, Renton, Sick Boy, Tommy, Lizzy and Begbie.

Begbie's story overlaps with the subsequent depiction of the incident.

BEGBIE
(voice-over)

Picture the scene. Wednesday morning in the Volley. Me and Tommy are playing pool. No problems, and I'm playing like Paul fucking Newman by the way. I'm giving the boy here the tanning of a lifetime. So anyway, it comes to the final ball, the deciding shot of the tournament: I'm on the black and he's sitting in the corner, looking all biscuit-arsed. Then this hard cunt comes in. Obviously fancied himself. Starts looking at me. Right fucking at me. Trying to put off, like, just for kicks. Looking at me as if to say, 'Come ahead, square go.' Well, you know me, I'm no looking for trouble but at the end of the day I'm the cunt with the pool cue and I'm game for a swedge. So I squared up, casual like. So what does the hard cunt do, or so-called hard cunt? Shites it. Puts down his drink, turns around and gets the fuck out of there. And after that, the game was mine.

*Cut from completed film.

INT. POOL HALL. DAY

The events in the pool hall, as described by Begbie.

Begbie and Tommy are playing pool.

Begbie is playing like a wizard.

Tommy looks defeated.

Lining up for the final ball, Begbie is distracted by a large Hard Man standing at the bar staring at him.

Begbie stands up and walks slowly towards the Hard Man.

They stand, eye to eye, for a moment.

Begbie swings the pool cue slowly into his palm.

The Hard Man turns and leaves.

Begbie drinks the Hard Man's pint, then pots the black with a brilliant shot.

INT. PUB 2. DAY

Begbie, his story complete, finishes his pint. The others continue to stare at him, frozen as though expecting something more. Begbie smiles and throws the pint glass over his head.

Freeze-frame: the glass in mid-air and Begbie's smiling face.

RENTON
(*voice-over*)

And that was it. That was Begbie's story. Or at least that was Begbie's version of the story. But a couple of days later I got the truth from Tommy. It was one of his major weaknesses: he never told lies, never took drugs, and never cheated on anyone.

INT. TOMMY'S FLAT. DAY

Renton's hand flicks through a long row of videos on the floor while the sound of weights being lifted (by Tommy) emanates from nearby.

Most of the videos are feature films or comedy shows, some with titles written in Tommy's hand, but two catch Renton's attention.

They are 100 Great Goals *and* Tommy and Lizzy, Vol. 1, *the latter a handwritten title.*

Renton looks from the videos round to Tommy, who is engrossed in lifting weights.

TOMMY

Well, sure it was Wednesday morning, we were in the Volley playing pool, that much is true.

INT. POOL HALL. DAY

Tommy's account over a depiction of his version.

TOMMY
(voice-over)

But Begbie is playing absolutely fucking gash. He's got a hangover so bad he can hardly hold the fucking cue, never mind pot the ball. I'm doing my best to lose, trying to humour him, like, but it's not doing any good: every time I touch the ball I pot something, every time Begbie goes near the table he fucks it up. So he's got the hump, right, but finally I manage to set it up so all he's got to do is pot the black to win one game and salvage a little pride and maybe not kick my head in, right. So he's on the black, pressure shot, and it all goes wrong, big time. What does he do? Picks on this specky wee gadge at the bar and accuses him of putting him off by looking at him. Can you believe it? I mean, the poor cunt hasn't even glanced in our direction. He's sitting there quiet as a mouse when Beggars gubs him with the cue. He was going to chib him, I tell you, then I thought he was going to do me. The Beggar is fucking psycho, but he's a mate, you know, so what can you do?

The events are as follows:

Begbie and Tommy are playing pool.

Begbie, furious, miscues, goes in off, etc.

Tommy deliberately misses sitters and tries to look annoyed.

Begbie lines up to play the black. It is unmissable.

At the bar beyond sits a harmless young Man, wearing the same clothes as the Hard Man in Begbie's account except that they are now

26

baggy rather than taut. He is clearly not staring at Begbie but drinks a half-pint and eats some crisps.

As Begbie plays, the Man bites a crisp.

Begbie miscues, rips the cloth and the ball flies off the table.

Tommy catches it and looks up to see Begbie assaulting the young Man.

Tommy cautiously restrains Begbie as he reaches into his jacket for a knife.

Begbie turns and for a moment looks as though he might attack Tommy.

INT. TOMMY'S FLAT. DAY

Tommy puts down his weights.

Renton holds up 100 Great Goals.

RENTON

Can I borrow this one?

INT. PUB 2. NIGHT

The freeze-frame of the glass in mid-air and Begbie's smiling face.

RENTON
(*voice-over*)

Yeah, the guy's a psycho, but it's true, he's a mate as well, so what can you do? Just stand back and watch and try not to get involved. Begbie didn't do drugs either, he just did people. That's what he got off on: his own sensory addiction.

The glass falls into the crowd.

Screaming starts. A Woman is bleeding from a wound in her head. The Men beside her turn furiously around to look for the source of the glass.

Up on the balcony, Begbie stands up. The screams and shouting continue below.

Begbie appears at the bottom of the staircase down from the balcony.

He strides towards the bleeding Woman and begins shouting.

> BEGBIE

All right. Nobody move. The girl got glassed and no cunt leaves here until we find out which cunt did it.

A Man stands up from one of the tables.

> MAN

And who the fuck do you think you are?

Begbie kicks the Man in the groin. Another moves towards him but is blocked by the Men surrounding the girl. Soon the whole mass dissolves into a brutal scrum, in which Begbie plays a prominent part.

Up on the balcony, the rest of the gang watch in silence.

INT. RENTON'S FLAT. DAY

The empty cover for 100 Great Goals *lies on the floor.*

Sick Boy and Renton sit dispassionately watching Tommy and Lizzy in their home-made soft-porn video.

> RENTON
> (voice-over)

And as I sat watching the intimate and highly personal video, stolen only hours earlier from one of my best friends, I realized that something important was missing from my life.

INT. CLUB. NIGHT

A mass of dancing bodies fills the floor. The music is very loud.

At the side of the dance floor sit Tommy and Spud. They look rather gloomy. There is an empty seat beside each of them. Spud is drinking heavily.

Tommy turns and speaks to Spud. His lips move but nothing is audible. Spud is not even aware that Tommy has spoken.

Tommy bellows in Spud's ear.

Tommy's words and all subsequent conversation in the dance area of the

club appear as subtitles, the characters' communications somewhere
between speech and mime.

TOMMY

How's it going with Gail?

SPUD

No joy yet.

TOMMY

How long is it?

SPUD

Six weeks.

TOMMY

Six weeks!

SPUD

It's a nightmare. She told me she didn't want our relationship to
start on a physical basis as that is how it would be principally
defined from then on in.

TOMMY

Where did she come up with that?

29

SPUD

She read it in *Cosmopolitan*.

TOMMY

Six weeks and no sex?

SPUD

I've got balls like watermelons, I'm telling you.

INT. NIGHTCLUB, WOMEN'S TOILET. NIGHT

Gail and Lizzy are smoking and talking.

GAIL

I read it in *Cosmopolitan*.

LIZZY

It's an interesting theory.

GAIL

Actually it's a nightmare. I've been desperate for a shag, but watching him suffer was just too much fun. You should try it with Tommy.

LIZZY

What, and deny myself the only pleasure I get from him? Did I tell you about my birthday?

GAIL

What happened?

LIZZY

He forgot. Useless motherfucker.

INT. NIGHTCLUB. DANCE AREA. NIGHT

Tommy and Spud seated as before. Their words are subtitled.

As they are speaking Gail and Lizzy return and sit down.

TOMMY

Useless motherfucker, that's what she called me. I told her, I'm sorry, but these things happen. Let's put it behind us.

SPUD

That's fair enough.

30

TOMMY

Yes, but then she finds out I've bought a ticket for Iggy Pop the
same night.

SPUD

Went ballistic?

TOMMY

Big time. Absolutely fucking radge. 'It's me or Iggy Pop, time to
decide.'

SPUD

So what's it going to be?

TOMMY

Well, I've paid for the ticket.

GAIL and LIZZY

What are you two talking about?

TOMMY and SPUD

Football. What were you talking about?

GAIL and LIZZY

Shopping.

Standing nearby but apart from them is Renton.

*Renton notes Spud and Tommy with their partners, and across the
other side Sick Boy and Begbie are engaged in flirtatious conversation
with Two Women.*

RENTON
(*voice-over*)

The situation was becoming serious. Young Renton noticed the
haste with which the successful, in the sexual sphere as in all
others, segregated themselves from the failures.

Begbie and Sick Boy with the Two Women.

Renton standing among a group of lone nerds.

*Renton wades on to the dance floor, looking at countless women, all of
whom either turn away or are spoken for.*

(voice-over)

Heroin had robbed Renton of his sex drive, but now it returned with a vengeance. And as the impotence of those days faded into memory, grim desperation took hold in his sex-crazed mind. His post-junk libido, fuelled by alcohol and amphetamine, taunted him remorselessly with his own unsatisfied desire dot dot dot.

> *Renton notices one girl (Diane) walking on her own towards the door.*

> *A Man carrying two drinks catches up with her and walks backwards, talking to her.*

> *She says nothing. He blocks her way.*

> *She takes one drink and downs it, then the other, handing him back the empty glasses. She steps past him and walks on towards the door.*

(voice-over)

And with that, Mark Renton had fallen in love.

EXT. STREET. NIGHT

The Girl walks away from the club, scanning the street for a taxi, and hails one which stops just as Renton calls out.

RENTON

Excuse me, I don't mean to harass you, but I was very impressed by the capable and stylish manner in which you dealt with that situation. I thought to myself: she's special.

DIANE

Thanks.

RENTON

What's your name?

DIANE

Diane.

RENTON

Where are you going, Diane?

DIANE

I'm going home.

32

RENTON

Where's that?

DIANE

It's where I live.

RENTON

Great.

DIANE

What?

RENTON

I'll come back if you like, but I'm not promising anything.

Diane halts abruptly as a taxi pulls up.

DIANE

Do you find that this approach usually works, or, let me guess, you've never tried it before. In fact, you don't normally approach girls, am I right? The truth is that you're a quiet, sensitive type but if I'm prepared to take a chance I might just get to know the inner you: witty, adventurous, passionate, loving, loyal, a little bit crazy, a little bit bad, but, hey, don't us girls just love that?

RENTON

Eh –

DIANE

Well, what's wrong, boy? Cat got your tongue?

RENTON

I think I left something back at the –

The girl has disappeared into the back of the taxi.

Renton looks around.

TAXI DRIVER

Are you getting in or not, pal?

EXT. ROAD. NIGHT

The taxi motors along.

INT. TAXI. NIGHT

Renton and Diane are kissing passionately in the back.

EXT. STREET. NIGHT

Spud is pushed against the wall held by his lapels. He drinks from a bottle of beer in one hand.

GAIL

Do you understand?

  Spud nods drunkenly.

  Gail releases her grip.

Our relationship is not being redefined; it is developing in an appropriate, organic fashion. I expect you to be a considerate and thoughtful lover, generous but firm. Failure on your part to live up to these very reasonable expectations will result in swift resumption of a non-sex situation. Right?

  Spud drinks from a bottle in the other hand and says nothing but does not look too happy.

INT. TOMMY'S FLAT. NIGHT

Tommy and Lizzy kiss while Tommy unlocks the door.

INT. DIANE'S HOME, HALLWAY. NIGHT

In a darkened suburban hallway, the door opens and two figures enter.

RENTON

Diane.

DIANE

Ssshh!

RENTON

Sorry.

DIANE

Shut up.

  They walk through another door and close it behind them.

35

INT. TOMMY'S FLAT. NIGHT

Tommy and Lizzy kiss against the inside of the door, taking their outer clothes off.

INT. DIANE'S BEDROOM. NIGHT

By a pale bedside light, Diane and Renton undress.

INT. GAIL'S BEDROOM. NIGHT

Spud is lying unconscious on the bed. Gail stands over him.

GAIL

Wake up, Spud, wake up. Sex.

She kicks him. He moans.

Casual sex.

She kicks him again. He moans again.

You useless bastard. So let's see what I'm missing.

She begins undressing him.

INT. DIANE'S BEDROOM. NIGHT

Renton lies on his back while Diane rides above him.

INT. GAIL'S BEDROOM. NIGHT

Gail throws Spud's clothes to the floor and throws a blanket over him.

GAIL

Not much.

She switches out the light.

INT. TOMMY'S FLAT. NIGHT

Tommy and Lizzy now lie on the bed in a state of semi-undress.

LIZZY

Tommy, let's put the tape on.

TOMMY

Now?

LIZZY

Yes, I want to watch ourselves while we're screwing.

TOMMY

Fuck, OK.

Tommy gets up and reaches into the row of videos on the floor. He lifts out Tommy and Lizzy, Vol. 1 *and hastily shoves it into the video.*

Tommy sits back on the bed with the remote control and presses 'play' as Lizzy kisses him.

His face registers consternation.

On the television, Archie Gemmill scores his famous goal against Holland in 1978.

INT. DIANE'S BEDROOM. NIGHT

Renton and Diane climax together.

Diane immediately climbs off and wraps herself in a robe.

RENTON

Christ, I haven't felt that good since Archie Gemmill scored against Holland in 1978.

DIANE

Right. You can't sleep here.

RENTON

What?

DIANE

Out.

RENTON

Come on.

DIANE

No argument. You can sleep on the sofa in the living room, or go home. It's up to you.

RENTON

Jesus.

DIANE

And don't make any noise.

INT. TOMMY'S FLAT. NIGHT

The lights are full on now. Lizzy sits on the bed clutching a blanket around herself.

Tommy hops around in his underwear, searching desperately.

All the videos are opened and scattered everywhere.

LIZZY

What do you mean, it's 'gone'? Where has it gone, Tommy?

TOMMY

It'll be here somewhere. I might have returned it by mistake.

LIZZY

Returned it? Where? To the video shop, Tommy? To the fucking video store? So every punter in Edinburgh is jerking off to our video? God, Tommy, I feel sick.

INT. DIANE'S HOME, LIVING-ROOM. MORNING

Renton lies submerged under a blanket.

The sounds of a normal morning travel from a room nearby: whistles, radio, voices.

Renton peeps over the edge of the blanket, then covers his head again.

INT. GAIL'S BEDROOM. MORNING

Spud opens his eyes. With his fingers, he feels crusted liquid around his mouth.

Abruptly he turns around: the bed is soaked in vomit.

He looks under the cover and drops it again in revulsion.

INT. DIANE'S HOME, LIVING-ROOM. DAY

Renton pulls himself up off the sofa and dresses as quickly as possible.

INT. GAIL'S BEDROOM. DAY

Spud wipes the vomit from his chest with a pillowcase, which he dumps in the middle of the sheets before gathering the whole lot up as a bundle.

INT. DIANE'S HOME, HALL/KITCHEN. DAY

The door swings open. A Man and Woman, about Renton's age, sit at the kitchen table. They look up to see Renton in the doorway.

                    MAN
Good morning.

                    WOMAN
Come in and sit down. You must be Mark.

  Renton walks to the table and sits down.

                    RENTON
Yes, that's me.

                    WOMAN
You're a friend of Diane's?

                    RENTON
More of a friend of a friend, really.

                    MAN
Right.

                    RENTON
Are you her flatmates?

  The couple exchange a look and laugh.

                    WOMAN
Flatmates. I must remember that one.

  The Man and Woman look beyond Renton. He too turns and follows their gaze.

  Diane stands in the doorway.

39

She is wearing school uniform.

INT. GAIL'S HOME, HALL/KITCHEN. DAY

The door swings open to reveal the kitchen. Gail, her Father and Mother are seated around the table, eating breakfast.

They look towards Spud, who carries the knotted bundle of sheets as he approaches the table.

GAIL

Good morning, Spud.

SPUD

Morning, Gail. Morning, Mrs Houston, Mr Houston.

MOTHER

Morning, Spud. Sit down and have some breakfast.

SPUD

Sorry about last night –

GAIL

It's all right. I slept fine on the sofa.

SPUD

I had a little too much to drink. I'm afraid I had a slight accident.

FATHER

Oh, don't worry, these things happen. It does everyone good to cut loose once in a while.

GAIL

This one could do with being tied up once in a while.

MOTHER

I'll put the sheets in the washing machine just now.

SPUD

No, I'll wash them. I'll take them home and bring them back.

MOTHER

There's no need.

SPUD

It's no problem.

MOTHER

No problem for me either.

She advances to take the bundle. Spud steps back.

SPUD

Really, no.

MOTHER

Honestly, it's no problem.

SPUD

I'd really rather take care of it myself.

MOTHER

Spud, they're my sheets.

She takes hold of the bundle.

Spud does not yield.

She pulls harder. Spud holds on. She tugs powerfully.

The bundle bursts open with an explosion of vomit and excrement

41

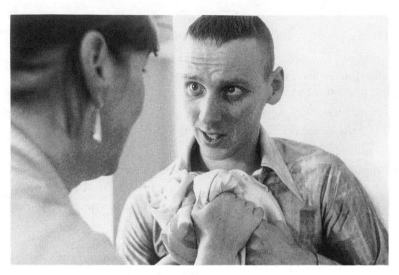

that covers everything in the kitchen.

Only Spud remains untouched.

*[SPUD
I guess this means I'll never get to have sex with Gail.

INT. TOMMY'S FLAT. DAY

Tommy sits alone, watching 100 Great Goals.]

EXT. STREET. DAY

Renton paces briskly down the street, followed by Diane.

                              DIANE
I don't see why not.

                              RENTON
Because it's illegal.

                              DIANE
Holding hands?

*Cut from completed film.

RENTON

No, not holding hands.

DIANE

In that case you can do it. You were quite happy to do a lot more last night.

RENTON

And that's what's illegal. Do you know what they do to people like me inside? They'd cut my balls off and flush them down the fucking toilet.

They stop at the school gates.

DIANE

Calm down. You're not going to jail.

RENTON

Easy for you to say.

DIANE

Can I see you again?

RENTON

Certainly not.

Renton walks away.

DIANE

If you don't see me again I'll tell the police.

Renton turns and walks back to her. They stand for a moment, then Renton walks away again. Diane smiles.

(*to herself*)

I'll see you around then.

EXT. VIDEO STORE. DAY

In the cold light of morning, Tommy and Lizzy wait, not speaking, outside the still-closed video store.

43

*[EXT. RAIL BRIDGE. DAY

A train speeds across.

INT. TRAIN. DAY

Sick Boy, Tommy, Spud and Renton sit drinking from an extensive carry-out.

SICK BOY

This had better be good.

TOMMY

It will be. It'll make a change for three miserable junkies who don't know what they want to do with themselves since they stopped doing smack.

SICK BOY

If I'm giving up a whole day and the price of a ticket, I'm just saying it had better be good. There's plenty of other things I could be doing.

TOMMY

Such as?

SICK BOY

Such as sitting in a darkened room, watching videos, drinking, smoking dope and wanking. Does that answer your question?

They sit in silence.]

EXT. STATION. DAY

The station is in the middle of a moor. There appears to be no habitation around. In the distance are some hills.

The train stands at the station.

As it pulls away, Renton, Spud, Tommy and Sick Boy are left standing on the platform, looking around.

SICK BOY

Now what?

*Cut from completed film.

TOMMY

We go for a walk.

SPUD

What?

TOMMY

A walk.

SPUD

But where?

Tommy points vaguely across the moor.

TOMMY

There.

SICK BOY

Are you serious?

They step across the tracks towards the vast moorland. They stop.

All but Tommy sit down on rocks or clumps of heather.

TOMMY

Well, what are you waiting for?

45

I don't know, Tommy. I don't know if it's . . . normal.

A group of three serious Walkers trudge past from the other end of the platform, decked out in regulation Berghaus from head to foot. They tramp off towards the wilderness. The boys watch them go.

Spud opens a can.

TOMMY

It's the great outdoors.

SICK BOY

It's really nice, Tommy. Can we go home now?

TOMMY

It's fresh air.

SICK BOY

Look, Tommy, we know you're getting a hard time off Lizzy, but there's no need to take it out on us.

TOMMY

Doesn't it make you proud to be Scottish?

RENTON

I hate being Scottish. We're the lowest of the fucking low, the scum of the earth, the most wretched, servile, miserable, pathetic trash that was ever shat into civilization. Some people hate the English, but I don't. They're just wankers. We, on the other hand, are colonized by wankers. We can't even pick a decent culture to be colonized by. We are ruled by effete arseholes. It's a shite state of affairs and all the fresh air in the world will not make any fucking difference.

The three serious Walkers are receding into the distance.

The boys troop back towards the platform.

(*voice-over*)

At or around this time, we made a healthy, informed, democratic decision to get back on drugs as soon as possible. It took about twelve hours.

INT. SWANNEY'S FLAT. DAY

Renton hands over money to Swanney.

Renton then begins cooking up.

Also present and cooking or shooting up are Spud, Swanney, Allison and Baby, and Sick Boy.

>   RENTON
>   *(voice-over)*
> It looks easy, this, but it's not. It looks like a doss, like a soft option, but living like this, it's a full-time business.

   He injects.

INT. SHOP. DAY

Renton, Spud and Sick Boy are stuffing objects into their shirts and pockets.

INT. SWANNEY'S FLAT. DAY

Renton lies back, narcotized.

EXT. STREET. DAY

Renton and Spud are running along the street.

Two uniformed Store Detectives are running after them.

Sick Boy stands in a doorway. As the Detectives run past, he strolls away in the opposite direction.

INT. SWANNEY'S FLAT. DAY

Renton lies back as before.

>   SICK BOY
> Ursula Andress was the quintessential Bond girl. That's what everyone says. The embodiment of his superiority to us: beautiful, exotic, highly sexual and yet unavailable to everyone but him. Shite. Let's face it: if she'd shag one punter from Edinburgh, she'd shag the fucking lot of us.

INT. SWANNEY'S FLAT. LATER

Spud cooks up, watched by Swanney.

Nearby lie the drugged forms of Renton, Sick Boy and Allison and Baby.

INT. RENTON FAMILY HOME, LIVING-ROOM. NIGHT

Renton's Mother and Father sit reading the paper and a magazine.

INT. RENTON FAMILY HOME, PARENTS' BEDROOM. NIGHT

Renton trawls through drawers and any containers (shoe boxes, make-up boxes, under the mattress, etc.) until he finds some cash/jewellery.

INT. SWANNEY'S FLAT. DAY

Renton lies back, staring vacantly ahead.

Tommy flops down beside him. Renton shows barely a flicker of awareness.

> TOMMY
> Lizzy's gone, Mark, she's gone and fucking dumped me. It was the video tape and that Iggy Pop business and all sorts of other stuff. She told me where to go and no mistake. I said, is there any chance of getting back together, like, but no way, no fucking way.

INT. HOSPITAL WARD SITTING-ROOM. DAY

A few elderly patients sit in armchairs watching daytime television.

Renton and Spud jump and climb through an open window. Watched by the helpless patients, they calmly disconnect the television and take it with them as they leave by the same route.

INT. SWANNEY'S FLAT. DAY

Renton and Tommy slumped side by side as before.

> TOMMY
> I want to try it, Mark. You're always going on about how it's the ultimate hit and that. Better than sex. Come on, I'm a fucking adult. I want to find out for myself.

Renton huddles up and leans away from Tommy.

I've got the money.

Tommy produces ten pounds from his pocket.

EXT. STREET. DAY

Renton and Spud run along the street.

INT. SWANNEY'S FLAT. DAY

Tommy lies drugged on the floor.

INT. FLAT TO BE BURGLED. DAY

The door of an ordinary flat is kicked open.

Begbie walks in, crowbar in hand, followed by Sick Boy and Spud.

INT. SWANNEY'S FLAT. DAY

                    SICK BOY
Honor Blackman a.k.a. Pussy Galore, what a total fucking
misnomer. I wouldn't touch her with yours. I'd sooner shag Col
Kreb. At least you know where you are with a woman like that.
Not much to look at, like, but personality, that's what counts,
that's what keeps a relationship going through the years. Like
heroin. I mean, heroin's got fucking great personality.

Sick Boy opens the heel of his shoe to reveal a syringe.

*[INT. FLAT TO BE BURGLED, LIVING-ROOM. DAY

Begbie and Sick Boy turn the flat over in search of anything to steal.]

INT. SWANNEY'S FLAT. DAY

*Swanney hands over a small bag of heroin in exchange for ten pounds
from Renton.*

*Cut from completed film.

*[INT. FLAT TO BE BURGLED, KITCHEN. DAY

Spud checks the fridge and pulls out a large chunk of deep-frozen meat.

He hits with the crowbar until it fractures and splits. Inside there is some jewellery.]

INT. CAR. DAY

The car is empty. A window is broken and the door opened.

The car alarm goes off.

Renton reaches under the seat and finds the radio/cassette. He then pulls the bonnet release.

EXT. CAR. DAY

The car alarm rings on until Renton calmly produces a pair of wire cutters and a spanner to cut free and release the battery.

The alarm is silenced.

Renton walks away with the battery and the stereo.

INT. GP'S SURGERY. DAY

RENTON
(*voice-over*)
Swanney taught us to adore and respect the National Health Service, for it was the source of much of our gear. We stole drugs, we stole prescriptions, or bought them, sold them, swapped them, forged them, photocopied them or traded them with cancer victims, alcoholics, old age pensioners, AIDS patients, epileptics and bored housewives. We took morphine, diamorphine, cyclozine, codeine, temazepam, nitrezepam, phenobarbitone, sodium amytal dextropropoxyphene, methadone, nalbuphine, pethidine, pentazocine, buprenorphine, dextromoramide chlormethiazole. The streets are awash with drugs that you can have for unhappiness and pain, and we took them all. Fuck it, we would have injected Vitamin C if only they'd made it illegal.

*Cut from completed film.

51

The GP examines Renton's chest and smiles.

The GP turns to wash his hands. Renton pulls on his shirt and steals a prescription pad off the desk.

★[INT. SWANNEY'S FLAT. DAY

Renton lies back with his eyes closed. A football enters the frame to bounce off his head and out again.

He opens his eyes and it happens again.

Opposite him, Spud, Sick Boy and Tommy stand looking down on him.

Tommy throws the ball again.]

INT. PUB I. DAY

It's the first day of the Edinburgh Festival.

Renton, Tommy, Spud, Sick Boy and Begbie sit drinking.

They observe a young male American Tourist walk in in a bulky red anorak and glasses. He goes past them towards the toilet.

Begbie stands up.

INT. PUB I, TOILET. DAY

The American Tourist turns from the urinal to see Begbie, Renton, Sick Boy, Spud and Tommy approaching. Begbie punches and kicks the Tourist and pulls out a knife.

★[INT. TAXI. DAY

The door of the taxi opens. Begbie, Tommy, Spud, Sick Boy and Renton get in, carrying the red anorak and glasses.

As the taxi pulls away they study the photograph in the passport. They look at one another in agreement.

★Cut from completed film.

EXT. TAXI. DAY

The taxi motors along.]

INT. PUB I. NIGHT

A man at the bar is now wearing the red anorak.

Begbie divides up the money among Sick Boy, Tommy, Spud and Renton.

Renton takes his share.

BEGBIE

And remember, Rents: no skag.

RENTON

Aye, OK, Franco.

RENTON
(voice-over)

But the good times couldn't last for ever.

INT. SWANNEY'S FLAT. DAY

Renton lies as before. Around the room are Swanney, Allison, Tommy, Spud and Sick Boy.

53

Allison begins screaming and wailing.

Slowly, the others rouse themselves to varying degrees.

RENTON
(*voice-over*)

I think Allison had been screaming all day, but it hadn't really registered before. She might have been screaming for a week for all I knew. It's been days since I've heard anyone speak, though surely someone must have said something in all that time, surely to fuck someone must have?

SICK BOY

What's wrong, Allison?

Allison points towards the bundle of dirty blankets in which her baby is wrapped. Sick Boy follows her directions.

SPUD

Calm down, calm down. It's going to be all right, everything's going to be just fine.

RENTON
(*voice-over*)

Nothing could have been further from the truth. In point of fact, nothing at all was going to be just fine. On the contrary, everything was going to be bad. Bad? I mean worse than it already was.

Sick Boy stands over the bundle. The baby is dead.

SICK BOY

Oh, fuck.

Sick Boy reaches out to Allison.

RENTON
(*voice-over*)

It wasn't my baby. She wasn't my baby. Baby Dawn. She wasn't mine. Spud's? Swanney's? Sick Boy's? I don't know. Maybe Allison knew. Maybe not. I wished I could think of something to say, something sympathetic, something human.

SICK BOY

Say something, Mark, say something –

RENTON

I'm cookin' up.

There is a silence.

Renton begins scrambling around through the works.

ALLISON

Cook one for me, Renton. I need a hit.

RENTON
(*voice-over*)

And so she did, I could understand that. To take the pain away. So I cooked up and she got a hit, but only after me. That went without saying.

EXT. STREET. DAY

Renton, Spud and Sick Boy cross the road to approach the shop.

RENTON
(*voice-over*)

Well, at least we knew who the father was now. It wasn't just the baby that died that day. Something inside Sick Boy was lost and never returned. It seemed he had no theory with which to explain a moment like this.

*[INT. SHOP. DAY

Renton, Spud and Sick Boy are stuffing their pockets, as seen before.

Renton's theft is interrupted by Diane's voice.

DIANE

Hello there, Mark.

Diane is standing just beside him.

What are you doing?

*Cut from completed film.

55

Renton is speechless, but a few stolen items fall from inside his jacket down to the floor.

Diane looks down.

Spud and Sick Boy start to snigger.

One of the Store Detectives become aware of the group. He starts walking towards them.

You didn't tell me you were a thief.

SPUD

Hey, go easy, lady. The boy's got a habit to support.

SICK BOY

Opium doesn't just grow on trees, you know.

A few more items fall from Renton's jacket as the Store Detective closes in.

Renton looks at Diane.]

EXT. STREET. DAY

Renton and Spud are running, pursued by the Two Store Detectives.

RENTON
(voice-over)

Nor did I. Our only response was to keep on going and fuck everything. Pile misery upon misery, heap it up on a spoon and dissolve it with a drop of bile, then squirt it into a stinking purulent vein and do it all over again. Keep on going: getting up, going out, robbing, stealing, fucking people over, propelling ourselves with longing towards the day it would all go wrong.

As seen in the opening scene, Renton is nearly hit by a car that screeches to a halt as he crosses a road.

He looks at the driver, at Spud running away and the Store Detectives approaching.

(voice-over)

Because no matter how much you stash or how much you steal, you never have enough. No matter how often you go out and rob and fuck people over, you always need to get up and do it all again.

Renton smiles and waits.

(voice-over)

Sooner or later, this sort of thing was bound to happen.

One of the Detectives runs straight past him, after Spud.

The other Detective crashes into Renton with a mighty punch in the stomach.

INT. COURT. DAY

Spud and Renton stand in the dock. Renton's Mother and Father, Sick Boy, Begbie and Spud's Mother (Mrs Murphy) are among those in the gallery.

The Sheriff delivers his sentence.

SHERIFF

. . . because shoplifting is theft, which is a crime, and, despite what you may believe, there is no such entity as victimless crime. Heroin addiction may explain your actions, but it does not excuse them. Mr Murphy, you are a habitual thief, devoid of regret or remorse. In sentencing you to six months' imprisonment my only worry is that it will not be long before we meet again. Mr Renton, I understand that you have entered into a programme of rehabilitation in an attempt to wean yourself away from heroin. The suspension of your sentence is conditional upon your continued cooperation with this programme. Should you stand guilty before me again, I shall not hesitate to impose a custodial sentence.

RENTON

Thank you, your honour. With God's help, I'll conquer this affliction.

The Sheriff and Renton stare at one another for a moment. Renton turns to look at Spud, then back towards the Sheriff, who is now leaving the court.

57

(*voice-over*)
What can you say? Well, Begbie had a phrase for it.

INT. PUB I. DAY

The pub is crowded. Around Renton are his Mother, Father, Begbie,
Sick Boy and Gav.

BEGBIE
It was fucking obvious that that cunt was going to fuck some cunt.

There is a round of nodding and 'poor Spud'ing. Everyone begins to
talk at once.

FATHER
I hope you've learned your lesson, son.

MOTHER
Oh, my son, I thought I was going to lose you there. You're
nothing but trouble to me, but I still love you.

BEGBIE
Clean up your act, sunshine. Cut that shite out for ever.

MOTHER

You listen to Francis, Mark, he's talking sense.

BEGBIE

Fucking right and I am. See, inside, you wouldn't last two fucking days.

SICK BOY

There's better things than the needle, Rents. Choose life.

He winks.

MOTHER

I remember when you were a baby, even then you would never do what you were told.

BEGBIE

But he pulled it off, clever bastard, and he got a result.

They laugh, then fall silent.

Renton turns around. Behind him stands Spud's mother.

RENTON

Mrs Murphy, I'm sorry about Spud. It wasn't fair, him going down and not me –

Tears in her eyes, Mrs Murphy turns and walks away.

Renton watches her go. Behind him Begbie shouts.

BEGBIE

It's no our fault. Your boy went down because he was a fucking smack-head and if that's not your fault, I don't know what is.

Begbie turns back to Renton.

Right. I'll get the drinks in.

He moves towards the bar.

Renton slips away.

Renton walks through the bar towards the toilets, then out of a back door.

59

EXT. YARD. DAY

Renton emerges into a narrow yard surrounded by a high wall. He looks around. The steel back gate is locked.

> RENTON
> (*voice-over*)

I wished I had gone down instead of Spud. Here I was surrounded by my family and my so-called mates and I've never felt so alone, never in all my puff. Since I was on remand they've had me on this programme, the state-sponsored addiction, three sickly sweet doses of methadone a day instead of smack. But it's never enough, and at the moment it's nowhere near enough. I took all three this morning and now I've got eighteen hours to go till my next shot and a sweat on my back like a layer of frost. I need to visit the mother superior for one hit, one fucking hit to get us over this long, hard day.

Renton climbs the wall. He stands on top, then dives off the other side, executing a somersault in mid-air.

INT. SWANNEY'S FLAT. NIGHT

Swanney is cooking up.

Renton lands on the floor behind him like a gymnast.

> RENTON

What's on the menu this evening?

> SWANNEY

Your favourite dish.

> RENTON

Excellent.

> SWANNEY

Your usual table, sir?

> RENTON

Why, thank you.

Renton sits on his usual cushion on the floor.

SWANNEY
And would sir care to settle his bill in advance?

RENTON
Stick it on my tab.

SWANNEY
Regret to inform, sir, that your credit limit was reached and
breached a long time ago.

RENTON
In that case –

He produces twenty pounds.

SWANNEY
Oh, hard currency, why, sir, that'll do nicely.

He swipes the notes underneath a UV forgery checker.

Can't be too careful when we're dealing with your type, can we?

Renton begins his search for a vein.

Would sir care for a starter? Some garlic bread perhaps?

RENTON
No, thank you. I'll proceed directly to the intravenous injection of
hard drugs, please.

SWANNEY
As you wish.

*He hands Renton the syringe. Renton injects, then lies back on the
dirty, red, carpeted floor.*

*He lies completely still. His pupils shrink. His breathing becomes slow,
shallow and intermittent.*

*He sinks into the floor until he is lying in a coffin-shaped and coffin-
sized pit, lined by the red carpet.*

Swanney stands over him.

SWANNEY
Perhaps sir would like me to call for a taxi?

An ambulance siren becomes faintly audible.

INT. SWANNEY'S STAIRWELL. NIGHT

The siren is a little louder.

Swanney holds Renton under his arms and drags him backwards down the steps.

EXT. STREET. NIGHT

As Swanney emerges, still dragging Renton, the siren grows louder and then an ambulance speeds by without stopping.

Swanney drags Renton across the pavement and into the open door of a waiting taxi.

Swanney then steps out of the taxi's other door, pausing only to tuck a ten-pound note into Renton's pocket before closing the door.

INT. TAXI. NIGHT

Renton lies on the floor of the taxi, as Swanney left him, rolling slightly as the taxi takes a corner.

EXT. HOSPITAL/TAXI. NIGHT

The taxi is stationary.

We do not see the driver's face but his hand opens the door and then drags Renton out on to the pavement by his ankles before taking the ten-pound note, getting back in the cab and driving away.

Renton lies on the pavement.

Two Porters lift him by arms and ankles on to a trolley.

We do not see the Porters' faces as they wheel Renton into the hospital.

INT. HOSPITAL ACCIDENT AND EMERGENCY DEPARTMENT. NIGHT

Renton is wheeled through the department, then into a bay surrounded by a white nylon curtain.

INT. TROLLEY BAY. NIGHT

The Porters lift Renton from one trolley on to another, then leave him alone in the bay surrounded by the curtain.

Renton lies alone. His breathing is still shallow and erratic. Around him is the usual accident and emergency paraphernalia: blood pressure machine, oxygen tap, bandages, etc.

A Doctor comes in and gives Renton an injection, then leaves.

DOCTOR

Wake up. Wake up.

Renton breathes more easily.

*[*The Two Porters return with another trolley. They lift Renton roughly on to it and wheel him away.*

INT. HOSPITAL CORRIDOR. NIGHT

The Porters wheel Renton along.

INT. WARD. NIGHT

The Porters lift Renton off the trolley and dump him on the bed.

A nurse sticks a thermometer in his mouth.

INT. WARD. DAY

Renton's Father and Mother lift Renton, now fully conscious, off the bed and dump him in a wheelchair.

INT. HOSPITAL CORRIDOR. DAY

Mother walks ahead. Behind her, Father pushes Renton in the wheelchair.]

INT. TAXI. DAY

Mother and Father sit either side of Renton.

*Cut from completed film.

INT. RENTON'S BEDROOM. DAY

Father shoves Renton on to the bed, then walks out past Mother, who looks at Renton for a moment before closing the door.

INT. OTHER SIDE OF RENTON'S BEDROOM DOOR. DAY

Renton's Father's hand slides three bolts across to lock the door.

INT. RENTON'S BEDROOM. DAY

Renton lies on the bed.

> RENTON
> (*voice-over*)

I don't feel the sickness yet, but it's in the post, that's for sure. I'm in the junky limbo at the moment, too ill to sleep, too tired to stay awake, but the sickness is on its way. Sweat, chills, nausea, pain and craving. Need like nothing else I have ever known will soon take hold of me. It's on its way.

> *The door opens. Renton's Mother walks in with a bowl of soup and a piece of bread. Father watches from the doorway.*

MOTHER

We'll help you, son. You'll stay with us until you get better. We'll beat this together.

RENTON

Maybe I could go back to the clinic.

MOTHER

No. No clinics, no methadone. That made you worse, you said so yourself. You lied to us, son, your own mother and father.

RENTON

At least get us some Temazepam.

MOTHER

No, you're worse coming off that than you are with heroin. Nothing at all.

FATHER

It's a clean break this time.

MOTHER

You're staying where we can keep an eye on you.

RENTON

I do appreciate what you're trying to do, I really do, but I need just one score, to ease myself off it. Just one. Just one.

Mother retreats past Father, who closes the door. The bolts go home again.

Renton lies back and closes his eyes. His forehead is damp with sweat.

He begins to shake.

He tosses and turns, becoming wrapped up in a swathe of blankets. As he unravels them, he is astonished to find a fully clothed Begbie in the bed with him.

BEGBIE

Well, this is a good laugh, you fucking useless bastard. Go on, sweat that shite out of your system, because if I come back and it's still there, I'll fucking kick it out.

Begbie laughs and covers himself up.

Renton rips away the blankets, but Begbie has gone.

Renton looks up.

Baby Dawn is crawling across the ceiling.

Renton looks down to see Diane sitting on the end of the bed.

Diane sings 'Temptation' by New Order.

DIANE

'Oh, you've got green eyes, oh, you've got red eyes, and I've never met anyone quite like you before.'

Renton looks back up. Dawn continues her slow crawl, leaving behind a thick trail of unidentifiable slime.

Renton looks down. Sick Boy sits on the end of the bed, holding a cup of tea and a chocolate biscuit.

Mother stands behind him.

SICK BOY

It's a mug's game, Mrs Renton. I'm not saying I was blameless myself, far from it, but there comes a time when you have to turn your back on that nonsense and just say no.

Sick Boy takes a bite of his biscuit.

Dawn crawls on. She has fangs now.

Spud sits on the end of the bed, in a caricature prison uniform with arrows on it, plus a ball and chain.

Dawn has claws as well.

Tommy sits on the end of the bed. He looks terrible.

TOMMY

Better than sex, Rents, better than sex. The ultimate hit. I'm a fucking adult. I'll find out for myself. Well, I'm finding out all right.

Renton looks up again just as the baby drops on to his face. He tears her off and throws her into a corner.

Renton's Mother and Father are washing him. Mother bends down and picks up the large, damp sponge from the corner, where it landed. She wipes her son's face with it.

FATHER

Mark, there's something you need to do.

*[INT. CONSULTING ROOM. DAY

A Doctor stands up as Renton enters.

DOCTOR

Come in. Sit down, please.

They both sit down.

Well, you've already spoken to one of our counsellors, but before we go on there're just a few questions I'd like to ask you.]

INT. RENTON FAMILY HOME, LIVING-ROOM. DAY

Renton, his Mother and Father sit watching television.

INT. STUDIO. DAY

Renton is sitting inside a plastic booth shaped like a giant syringe.

The Doctor, now dressed as a game-show host, stands in front, with Renton's Mother and Father beside him.

DOCTOR

Question number one: the human immunodeficiency virus is a – what?

FATHER

Retrovirus?

DOCTOR

Retrovirus is the correct answer.

Fanfare.

Question number two: HIV binds to which receptor on the host lymphocyte? Which receptor?

*Cut from completed film.

67

Mother and Father confer.

FATHER

CD4.

DOCTOR

CD4 receptor is the correct answer.

Fanfare.

And now, question number three: is he guilty or not guilty?

MOTHER

He's our son.

DOCTOR

Is the correct answer.

Fanfare.

And now it's time to 'Take the Test'.

Lights flash. Music. A garish Hostess walks on with two envelopes. She holds them out for Mother to choose one.

INT. CONSULTING ROOM. DAY

The Doctor watches in silence as the Hostess, now dressed as a medical technician, draws blood from Renton's arm and puts it in a tube. She marks the tube with a pre-printed, numbered label.

INT. STUDIO. DAY

Mother opens one of the envelopes. She is speechless with joy.

The plastic booth opens up. Lights flash again, etc.

Renton steps out.

INT. SOCIAL CLUB. NIGHT

Renton, his Mother and Father sit at a table in the local social club. It is a Saturday night and the club is busy.

Everyone sits in rapt silence. It is not initially clear what is going on. Near the bar a Caller with a microphone calls over the PA –

Two and four, twenty-four . . . seven . . . fifteen . . . clickety-click, sixty-six –

And so on, as he draws the numbers from the drum.

Everyone studies their cards, except Renton, who studies the people instead, his drink untouched.

The number-calling continues until suddenly interrupted by Mother's voice.

MOTHER

Mark . . . Mark, you've got a house. House! House! For goodness' sake, Mark.

They bustle around him and pass his card to the front.

RENTON
(*voice-over*)

It seems, however, that I really am the luckiest guy in the world. Several years of addiction right in the middle of an epidemic, surrounded by the living dead, but not me – I'm negative. It's official. And once the pain goes away, that's when the real battle starts. Depression. Boredom. You feel so fucking low, you'll want to fucking top yourself.

His mother counts a wad of money in front of him.

EXT. HOUSING ESTATE. DAY

On the door of a flat 'plaguer', 'HIV' and 'junky AIDS scum' are daubed on the walls.

The sound of a ball being regularly bounced against a wall can be heard.

INT. TOMMY'S FLAT. NIGHT

It is poorly furnished. Tommy is seated.

Renton has the football, which he kicks against the wall and catches, then drops and kicks again, and so on. The ball is slightly flat.

Are you getting out much?

No.

Following the game at all?

No.

No. Me neither.

Renton drops the ball. It rolls to a halt in the corner.

He sits down.

You take the test?

Aye.

Clear?

Aye.

That's nice.

I'm sorry, Tommy.

Have you got any gear on you?

No, I'm clean.

Well, sub us, then, mate. I'm expecting a rent cheque.

Renton produces some of his bingo win.

As he hands the notes over, their eyes and hands meet for a moment.

Tommy puts the money away.

Thanks, Mark.

                              RENTON
No problem.

                    (*voice-over*)
No problem – easy to say when it's some other poor cunt with
shite for blood.

*[INT. HOSPITAL. NIGHT

Renton walks along a corridor and into a ward.

INT. WARD. DAY

Sheets cover the lower half of Swanney in bed.

*They are thrown back to reveal the stump of an above-knee
amputation.*

*Cut from completed film.

SWANNEY

Surprise! Pa-pah!

Renton sits down and takes it in silence.

Hit the artery by mistake. Common enough error, or so the quack tells us, as though that's going to make my leg grow back. Still, it could have been worse, it could have been my fucking dick. And I tell you what, in this place you get looked after: clean sheets, regular meals and all the morphine you can eat.

RENTON

Great.

SWANNEY

And see when I get out of here. I've got plans. Going to get myself straightened out and head off to Thailand, where women really know how to treat a guy. See, out there you can live like a king if you've got white skin and a few crisp tenners in your pocket. No fucking problem.

RENTON

Sure.

SWANNEY

The strategy is this: get clean, get mobile, get into dealing, and this time next year I'll be watching the rising sun with a posse of oriental buttocks parked on my coupon.

RENTON

Sounds great, Swanney.

SWANNEY

Yeah.

RENTON

You'll have to send us a postcard.

SWANNEY

Sure will, pal, sure will.

EXT. PARK. DAY

Renton and Sick Boy are seated in their firing patch, sitting on plastic bags with beer, vodka, hash and the cassette player. The airgun is present as before but they are not making any use of it.

SICK BOY

Eughh. Sounds horrible.

RENTON

It wasn't that bad.

SICK BOY

Did he – you know?

RENTON

What?

SICK BOY

You know.

RENTON

No, he didn't make me touch it.

SICK BOY

Oh no, don't even mention it.

RENTON

He made me lick it.

SICK BOY

God, you're sick.

RENTON

And I got a stitch stuck between my teeth, jerked my head back and the whole fucking stump fell off.

SICK BOY

Cut it out.

RENTON

When are you going to visit him?

SICK BOY

Don't know. Maybe Thursday.

73

You're a real mate. And what about Tommy? Have you been to see him yet?

Sick Boy is silent. He stiffens as he avoids Renton's gaze. They shift fractionally apart.

Renton tuts.

SICK BOY

Fuck you. OK, so Tommy's got the virus. Bad news, big deal. The gig goes on, or hadn't you noticed? Swanney fucks his leg up. Well, tough shit, but it could have been worse.

RENTON

You're all heart.

SICK BOY

I know a couple of addicts. Stupid wee lassies. I feed them what they need. A little bit of skag to keep them happy while the punters line up at a fiver a skull. It's easy money for me. Not exactly a fortune, but I'm thinking, 'I should be coining it here.' Less whores, more skag. Swanney's right. Get clean, get into dealing, that's where the future lies. Set up some contacts, get a good load of skag, punt it, profit. What do you think?

RENTON

Fuck you.

SICK BOY

And I'll tell you why. Because I'm fed up to my back teeth with losers, no-hopers, draftpacks, schemies, junkies and the like. I'm getting on with life. What are you doing?]

INT. RENTON'S BEDSIT. NIGHT

Renton sits alone on the bed, making a joint and reading a book.

There is a knock at the door.

Renton answers the door.

Diane is standing in the common passageway in her school uniform.

They stand in silence for a moment.

                    RENTON
What do you want?

                    DIANE
Are you clean?

                    RENTON
Yes.

                    DIANE
Is that a promise, then?

                    RENTON
Yes, as a matter of fact, it is.

                    DIANE
Calm down, I'm just asking. Is that hash I can smell?

                    RENTON
No.

                    DIANE
I wouldn't mind a bit, if it is.

                    RENTON
Well, it isn't.

                    DIANE
Smells like it.

                    RENTON
You're too young.

                    DIANE
Too young for what?

   Renton looks in each direction along the empty passageway.

INT. RENTON'S BEDSIT. NIGHT

Renton and Diane are lying in the bed.

Diane, wearing one of Renton's T-shirts, is rolling a mega-joint quite unaware of the scrutiny of Renton.

75

DIANE

You're not getting any younger, Mark. The world is changing,
music is changing, even drugs are changing. You can't stay in here
all day dreaming about heroin and Ziggy Pop.

RENTON

It's Iggy Pop.

DIANE

Whatever. I mean, the guy's dead anyway.

RENTON

Iggy Pop is not dead. He toured last year. Tommy went to see
him.

DIANE

The point is, you've got to find something new.

Diane completes the joint.

RENTON
(*voice-over*)

She was right. I had to find something new. There was only one
thing for it.

EXT. LONDON. DAY

*A contemporary retake of all those 'Swinging London' montages: Red
Routemaster/Trafalgar Square/Big Ben/Royalty/City gents in suits/
Chelsea ladies/fashion victims/Piccadilly Circus at night.*

*Intercut with close-ups of classic street names on a street map (all the
ones made famous by Monopoly).*

INT. ESTATE AGENT'S OFFICE. DAY

*The montage ends on one street, then draws back to reveal the whole
map of London pinned to a wall.*

*A Man holding a telephone walks in front of the map and belches
loudly.*

*Revealing more, he is in a scruffy, cramped office with half a dozen
occupied desks and twice as many telephones. Seated at the one nearest*

to the belching Man is Renton. He is wearing a shirt and tie now. He turns in response to the belch.

MAN

Can you take this call?

Renton takes the telephone and reaches for a piece of paper from which he reads.

RENTON

Hello, yes, certainly. It's a beautifully converted Victorian town house. Ideally located in a quiet road near to local shops and transport.

Renton checks his watch.

EXT. THE AI IN NORTH LONDON. DAY

Renton stands waiting beside this busy London road, outside some very unfortunate housing, as the traffic streams past.

RENTON
(*voice-over*)

Two bedrooms and a kitchen/diner. Fully fitted in excellent decorative order. Lots of storage space. All mod cons. Three hundred and twenty pounds per week.

A couple approach.

Renton unlocks the door of a flat and holds the door open while he ushers them in.

INT. LONDON FLAT. DAY

Renton shows the Couple round a typical London flat nightmare. A poor conversion, poor decor, everything small and ill-fitting. The windows rattle as the traffic roars by.

RENTON
(*voice-over*)

I settled in not too badly and I kept myself to myself. Sometimes, of course, I thought about the guys, but mainly I didn't miss them at all. After all, this was boom town where any fool could make cash from chaos and plenty did. I quite enjoyed the sound of it all.

Profit, loss, margins, takeovers, lending, letting, subletting, subdividing, cheating, scamming, fragmenting, breaking away. There was no such thing as society and even if there was, I most certainly had nothing to do with it. For the first time in my adult life I was almost content.

INT. LONDON BEDSIT. NIGHT

Renton finishes eating a pot noodle. He puts it down and picks up a letter. He lies back and reads.

Intercut with:

INT. SCHOOLROOM. DAY

A class is in progress. A teacher lectures to a mixed class, but Diane is not listening as she is writing.

EXT. SCHOOL DAY

Diane is leaving the school when Sick Boy catches up with her. They stop and then she walks away.

EXT. PARK. DAY

Diane walks along a concrete path. As she does so she has to step over Spud, who lies asleep/unconscious beside the remains of a carry-out.

DIANE
(voice-over)

Dear Mark, I'm glad you've found a job and somewhere to live. School is fine at the moment. I'm not pregnant but thanks for asking. Your friend Sick Boy asked me last week if I would like to work for him but I told him where to go. I met Spud, who sends his regards, or at least I think that's what he said. No one has seen Tommy for ages. And finally, Francis Begbie has been on television a lot this week –

INT. LONDON BEDSIT. NIGHT

Renton turns the page

DIANE
(*voice-over*)

as he is wanted by the police in connection with an armed
robbery in a jeweller's in Corstorphine. Take care. Yours with
love, Diane.

*There is a buzz at the door. Renton re-examines the letter. There is
another buzz.*

RENTON

Oh no.

INT. HALLWAY OUTSIDE BEDSIT. NIGHT

Renton opens the door to an unseen figure. It is Begbie.

INT. BEDSIT. NIGHT

*Renton sits on the bed. Begbie stands over him, pointing a gun at his
head.*

He pulls the trigger. It clicks harmlessly.

BEGBIE

Armed robbery? With a replica? How can it be armed robbery? It's
a fucking scandal.

*He 'fires' the gun a few times at his own head, then chucks it to the
floor.*

And the haul. Look.

He digs a few rings out of his pocket and throws them to Renton.

Solid silver, my arse. I took it to a fence – it's trash, pure trash.
There's young couples investing all their hopes in that stuff, and
what are they getting?

RENTON

It's a scandal, Franco.

BEGBIE

Too right it is. Now look, have you got anything to eat, 'cos I'm
fucking Lee Marvin, by the way.

INT. BEDSIT. DAY

Begbie is sitting on the bed in his underwear, eating cereal while watching television. A small carry-out is nearby.

Renton finishes dressing for work. He pauses at the open door, looking back towards his guest.

> RENTON
> (*voice-over*)

Begbie settled in in no time at all.

> *Begbie opens a can of beer. Renton closes the door.*

INT. HALLWAY OUTSIDE BEDSIT. DAY

Renton closes his door. He is about to walk away when he hears Begbie shouting.

> BEGBIE
> (*from the bedsit*)

Rents, Rents, come fucking back here.

> *Renton opens the door. Begbie is holding out an empty packet of cigarettes.*

Look.

> RENTON

What?

> BEGBIE

I've no fucking cigarettes.

> *Begbie throws the packet down to the floor. It lands near the door. He has turned back to the television and takes a swig of beer.*

> RENTON

Right.

> *Renton closes the door again.*

INT. BEDSIT. NIGHT

Renton and Begbie lie in the single bed with their heads at opposite ends.

Begbie snores. Renton is wide awake, with a pair of smelly-socked feet only inches from his nose.

> RENTON
> *(voice-over)*

Yeah, the guy's a psycho, but it's true, he's a mate as well, so what can you do?

INT. LONDON BEDSIT. DAY

Where the first empty packet of cigarettes fell to the floor there is now a large heap of empty packets: the product of weeks at sixty a day.

Another one lands on the pile.

Begbie, still in his underwear, still can in hand, sits watching the racing as before.

Behind him, cigarettes and alcohol are stacked up like a miniature duty-free warehouse.

Renton sits behind him, reading a book.

> BEGBIE

Hey, I'm wanting a bet put on.

> RENTON

Can you not go yourself?

> BEGBIE

I'm a fugitive from the law. I can't be seen on the fucking streets. Now watch my lips. Kempton Park. Two-thirty. Five pounds to win. Bad Boy.

INT. HALLWAY OUTSIDE BEDSIT. DAY

The door opens, Renton walks out, the door closes and Renton walks away.

A wild, frightening scream erupts from beyond the door.

INT. LONDON BEDSIT. DAY

Begbie, alone in the bedsit, is screaming a cry of primal joy.

RENTON
(*voice-over*)

Bad Boy came in at 16 to 1. And with the winnings, we went out to celebrate.

INT. LONDON PARTY. NIGHT

To loud music and strobing, fractured lights, surrounded by dry ice, Begbie dances near a tall woman.

Other people dance nearby.

Begbie gives the thumbs-up to Renton, who sits on a stool at one side drinking from a bottle of beer. Begbie and the Woman walk away.

Renton looks around the club at the various men and women.

RENTON
(*voice-over*)

Diane was right. The world is changing, music is changing, drugs are changing, even men and women are changing. One thousand years from now there'll be no guys and no girls, just wankers. Sounds great to me. It's just a pity that no one told Begbie.

EXT. STREET. NIGHT

A car sits in a street near the club, windows steamed up.

INT. CAR. NIGHT

Begbie and the Woman embrace passionately.

The Woman undoes Begbie's trousers.

INT. PARTY. NIGHT

Renton's gaze continues to wander around.

RENTON
(*voice-over*)

You see, if you ask me, we're heterosexual by default, not by decision. It's just a question of who you fancy.

INT. CAR. NIGHT

Begbie and the Woman continue their embrace as she unbuttons his shirt.

> RENTON
> (*voice-over*)

It's all about aesthetics and it's fuck all to do with morality.

> *Suddenly Begbie freezes. He is holding the 'Woman's' groin. There is something there that shouldn't be.*

> *Begbie goes crazy, simultaneously trying to put his clothes back on, hit the Woman and get out of the car.*

EXT. STREET. NIGHT

Begbie stumbles away from the car, pulling up his trousers as he goes.

> RENTON
> (*voice-over*)

But you try telling Begbie that.

INT. BEDSIT. NIGHT

Begbie sits on the bed.

Renton is sitting on the floor watching.

> BEGBIE

I'm no a fucking buftie and that's the end of it.

> RENTON

Let's face it, it could have been wonderful.

> *Begbie leaps off the bed, grabs Renton and head-butts him, then holds him by the lapel.*

> BEGBIE

Now, listen to me, you little piece of junky shit. A joke's a fucking joke, but you mention that again and I'll cut you up. Understand?

> *Begbie produces his knife.*

> *There is a knock at the door.*

They do not move.

There is another knock.

INT. BEDSIT. NIGHT

Begbie lies sleeping on the bed. There are two sets of feet by his head, one on each side.

At the other end lie Renton (awake) and Sick Boy (asleep).

RENTON
(voice-over)

Since I last saw him, Sick Boy had reinvented himself as a pimp and a pusher and was here to mix business and pleasure, setting up 'contacts', as he constantly informed me, for the great skag deal that was one day going to make him rich.

*[INT. ESTATE AGENT'S OFFICE. DAY

Renton sits at his desk, haggard and tired.

Other people bustle around him. Telephones ring, etc.

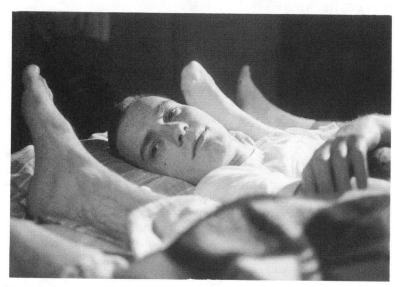

*Cut from completed film.

In the background the Man (who belched) is trying to promote a flat down the telephone.

MAN

Beautifully converted Victorian town house. Ideally located in a quiet road near to local shops and transport. Two bedrooms and a kitchen/diner. Fully fitted in excellent decorative order. Lots of storage space. All mod cons. Three hundred and twenty pounds per week.]

INT. BEDSIT. NIGHT

Renton (still dressed for work), Begbie and Sick Boy sit in a line on the bed with fish suppers laid out on their laps, but Renton's is untouched.

SICK BOY

Good chips.

RENTON

I can't believe you did that.

SICK BOY

I got a good price for it. Rents, I need the money.

RENTON

It was my fucking television.

SICK BOY

Well, Christ, if I'd known you were going to get so humpty about it, I wouldn't have bothered. Are you going to eat that?

He takes Renton's fish supper and adds it to his own.

Have you got a passport?

RENTON

Why?

SICK BOY

Well, this guy I've met runs a hotel. Brothel. Loads of contacts. Does a nice little sideline in punting British passports to foreigners. Get you a good price.

RENTON

Why would I want to sell my passport?

SICK BOY

It was just an idea.

INT. LEFT LUGGAGE ROOM. DAY

Renton drops his passport into an envelope and throws the envelope into a locker.

He turns the key and pockets it.

RENTON
(*voice-over*)

I had to get rid of them. Sick Boy didn't do his drug deal and he didn't get rich. Instead, he and Begbie just hung around my bedsit looking for things to steal. I decided to put them in the worst place in the world.

EXT. BUSY LONDON ROAD. DAY

Traffic floods past as before.

INT. LONDON FLAT. DAY

Inside the flat that Renton showed the couple around.

Sick Boy and Begbie are standing in the hallway.

Renton is in the open doorway. He throws them the keys and leaves.

INT. LONDON BEDSIT. NIGHT

The cramped bedsit is a mess, filled with litter and unwashed clothes.

Renton lies on his bed, content to be alone.

INT. LONDON FLAT. NIGHT

The flat is in darkness. The door opens and a figure enters. It is the Man from Renton's office.

RENTON
(*voice-over*)

But, of course, they weren't paying any rent, so when my boss found two desperate suckers who would, Sick Boy and Begbie were bound to feel threatened.

Man is followed by another couple.

He switches on a light.

MAN

As you can see, it's a beautiful conversion. Two bedrooms, kitchen/diner. Fully fitted. Lots of storage. All mod cons. Three hundred and twenty quid a week.

From nowhere, Begbie and Sick Boy spring out at him.

*[INT. BEDSIT. DAY

Renton looks around the stripped, empty bedsit one last time before closing the door as he leaves.]

RENTON
(*voice-over*)

And that was that. But by then we had another reason to go back. Tommy.

EXT. RAILWAY. DAY

An InterCity train speeds by.

INT. TOMMY'S FLAT. NIGHT

A kitten sits on the floor.

GAV
(*voice-over*)

Tommy knew he had the virus, like, but never knew he'd gone full-blown.

*Cut from completed film.

RENTON
(*voice-over*)
What was it, pneumonia or cancer?

GAV
(*voice-over*)
No, toxoplasmosis. Sort of like a stroke.

RENTON
(*voice-over*)
Eh? How's that?

INT. CREMATORIUM CHAPEL. DAY

A service is in progress. Those present include Renton and Gav, who are engaged in hushed conversation, Begbie, Spud, Sick Boy and Lizzy.

GAV
He wanted to see Lizzy again.

He indicates Lizzy.

Lizzy wouldn't let him near the house. So he bought a present for her, brought her a kitten.

RENTON
I bet Lizzy told him where to put it.

GAV
Exactly. I'm not wanting a cat, she says. Get to fuck, right. So there's Tommy stuck with this kitten. You can imagine what happened. The thing was neglected, pissing and shitting all over the place. Tommy was lying around fucked out of his eyeballs on smack or downers. He didn't know you could get toxoplasmosis from cat shit.

RENTON
I didn't either. What the fuck is it?

GAV
Fucking horrible. Like an abscess on your brain.

RENTON
Fucking hell. So what happened?

88

INT. TOMMY'S FLAT. DAY

The kitten as before.

Slow track back to reveal more.

> GAV
> (*voice-over*)

He starts getting headaches, so he just uses more smack, for the pain, like. Then he has a stroke. A fucking stroke. Just like that. Got home from hospital and died about three weeks later. Been dead for ages before the neighbours complained about the smell and the police broke the door down. Tommy was lying face down in a pool of vomit.

> *The lower half of Tommy's clothed body is visible.*

INT. CREMATORIUM CHAPEL. DAY

The coffin travels away. Gav and Renton watch it go.

> GAV

The kitten was fine.

INT. PUB I. NIGHT

Gav, Renton, Spud, Sick Boy, Begbie and a few others are gathered in the pub, still dressed in their funeral garb. They are drinking and talking.

*[SPUD

Every time I think of Tommy I think of Australia, because every time I went round he was just lying there, junked out of his mind, watching Aussie soaps. Until he sold the telly, of course, then he was just lying there. But every time I think of him I still think of Australia.]

> *There is a short silence before Spud begins softly singing 'Two Little Boys'. He finishes unaccompanied.*

*Cut from completed film.

89

INT. SWANNEY'S FLAT. NIGHT

Spud, Begbie and Renton are seated.

Sick Boy is handing round bottles of beer before he too sits down.

They are all still wearing their funeral garb.

Renton raises his bottle.

RENTON

Tommy.

They all drink.

SICK BOY

Did you tell him?

BEGBIE

No. On you go.

RENTON

What?

SICK BOY

There's a mate of Swanney's. Mikey Forrester – you know the guy. He's come into some gear. A lot of gear.

RENTON

How much?

SICK BOY

About four kilos. So he tells me. Got drunk in a pub down by the docks last week, where he met two Russian sailors. They're fucking carrying the stuff. For sale there and then, like. So he wakes up the next morning, realizes what he's done and gets very fucking nervous. Wants rid of this. *[He's looking for Swanney to punt it, but Swanney's nowhere to be seen since he lost his leg.]

RENTON

So?

SICK BOY

So he met me and I offered to take it off his hands at a very

*Cut from completed film.

reasonable price, with the intention of punting it on myself to a guy I know in London.

RENTON

So we've just come from Tommy's funeral and you're telling me about a skag deal?

BEGBIE

Yeah.

There is silence.

RENTON

What was your price?

SICK BOY

Four grand.

RENTON

But you don't have the money?

SICK BOY

We're two thousand short.

RENTON

That's tough.

SICK BOY

Come on, Mark, every cunt knows you've been saving up down in London.

RENTON

Sorry, boys, I don't have two thousand pounds.

BEGBIE

Yes, you fucking do. I've seen your statement.

RENTON

Jesus.

BEGBIE

Two thousand, one hundred and thirty-three pounds.

RENTON

Four kilos. That's what – ten years' worth? Russian sailors? Mikey Forrester? What the fuck are you on these days? You've been to jail, Spud, so what's the deal – like it so much you want to go back again?

SPUD

I want the money, Mark, that's all.

BEGBIE

If everyone keeps their mouth shut, there'll be no one going to jail.

*[EXT. STREET. DAY

Renton is visible first, apparently talking to himself, then Diane.

RENTON

It's so simple. We buy it at four grand, we punt it at twenty to this guy that Sick Boy knows, and he punts it on at sixty. Everyone's happy, everyone's in profit. I put up two. I come away with six.

DIANE

Unless you get caught.

RENTON

So long as everyone keeps their mouths shut, we'll not be getting caught.

DIANE

So why have you told me about it?

RENTON

Well, you're not going to tell anyone, are you, and besides, I thought we could meet up afterwards, maybe go somewhere together.

DIANE

I've got a boyfriend, Mark.

RENTON

What? steady like?

DIANE

That's right: 'going steady' for four weeks now.

*Cut from completed film.

RENTON

And what age are you? Thirteen? Fourteen?

DIANE

Sixteen next month.

RENTON

Happy birthday.

DIANE

What do you think – I should be carrying a torch for you?

Renton thinks it over.

RENTON

So what's he like?

DIANE

Well, he's young and he's healthy.

They both laugh.

And you're such a deadbeat, Mark.]

INT. SWANNEY'S FLAT. DAY.

Heroin is in the process of being prepared for injection: heated, drawn up, etc.

An arm is prepared for injection: sleeve rolled up, tourniquet bound, veins tapped, etc.

Mikey Forrester, Sick Boy, Spud and Begbie look on.

RENTON
(*voice-over*)

I hadn't told anyone everything that was running through my mind about what might happen in London. There were a lot of possibilities I didn't want to talk to anyone about. Ideas best kept to myself. What no one told me was that when we bought the skag, some lucky punter would have to try it out. Begbie didn't trust Spud and Sick Boy was too careful these days, so I rolled up my sleeve and did what had to be done.

Renton injects the heroin into a vein in his arm.

93

RENTON

It's good, it's fucking good.

*[EXT. BUS STATION. NIGHT

Renton walks past a Beggar huddling against a wall.

The Beggar's sign reads: 'FALKLANDS VETERAN. I LOST MY
LEG FOR MY COUNTRY. PLEASE HELP.'

The beggar is Swanney.]

RENTON
(*voice-over*)

Yes, that hit was good. I promised myself another one before I got
to London – just for old time's sake, just to piss Begbie off.

EXT. ROAD. NIGHT

The bus travels towards London.

INT. BUS NIGHT

Sick Boy dabs at amphetamine.

Spud drinks.

INT. BUS TOILET. NIGHT

Renton cooks up in the bus toilet.

RENTON
(*voice-over*)

This was to be my final hit. But let's be clear about this: there's
final hits and final hits. What kind was this to be? *[Some final hits
are actually terminal one way or another, while others are merely
transit points as you travel from station to station on the junky
journey through a junky life.]

*Cut from completed film.

94

INT. BUS. NIGHT

Begbie sits grimly. The others are relaxed.

RENTON
(*voice-over*)

This was his nightmare. The dodgiest scam in a lifetime of dodgie scams being perpetrated with three of the most useless and unreliable fuck-ups in town. I knew what was going on in his mind: any trouble in London and he would dump us immediately, one way or another. He had to. If he got caught with a bag full of skag, on top of that armed robbery shit, he was going down for fifteen to twenty. Begbie was hard, but not so hard that he didn't shite it off twenty years in Saughton.

BEGBIE

Did you bring the cards?

SICK BOY

What?

BEGBIE

The cards. The last thing I said to you was mind the cards.

SICK BOY

Well, I've not brought them.

BEGBIE

It's fucking boring after a while without the cards.

SICK BOY

I'm sorry.

BEGBIE

Bit fucking late, like.

SICK BOY

Well, why didn't you bring them?

BEGBIE

Because I fucking told you to do that, you doss cunt.

SICK BOY

Christ.

EXT. LONDON. DAY

The bus travels through London.

EXT. STREET. DAY

The gang enter a cheap hotel. Begbie's bag contains the heroin.

INT. HOTEL. DAY

They are met by Andreas, a man in his late thirties of Mediterranean appearance.

He shakes Sick Boy's hand.

ANDREAS
These are your friends?

SICK BOY
These are the guys I told you about.

ANDREAS
OK.

SICK BOY
Is he here?

97

ANDREAS

Yes, he's here. I hope you didn't get followed or nothing.

BEGBIE

We didn't get followed.

Andreas leads them along a corridor and into a room.

INT. HOTEL ROOM. DAY

An unexceptional Man is waiting.

Andreas leaves the room and closes the door.

Begbie opens the bag and produces the two slabs of heroin.

The Man opens both and tastes the heroin.

He produces a set of kitchen scales from his bag and weighs the two bags.

RENTON
(*voice-over*)

Straight away he clocked us for what we were: small-time wasters with an accidental big deal.

MAN

So what do you want for it?

BEGBIE

Twenty thousand.

MAN

But it's not worth more than fifteen.

BEGBIE

Nineteen.

The man shakes his head and lights a cigarette.

MAN

Nineteen I can't offer you, I'm sorry.

RENTON
(*voice-over*)

This was a real drag to him. He didn't need to negotiate. I mean,

what the fuck were we going to do if he didn't buy it? Sell it on the
streets? Fuck that.

*The deal is done. The Man hands over the money and waits as it is
counted, then leaves with the drugs.*

(voice-over)

We settled on sixteen thousand pounds. He had a lot more in the
suitcase, but it was better than nothing. And just for a moment it
felt really great, like we were all in it together, like friends, like it
meant something. A moment like that, it can touch you deep
inside, but it doesn't last long, not like sixteen thousand pounds.

INT. LONDON PUB. DAY

The pub is crowded with afternoon drinkers.

*Renton, Spud, Sick Boy and Begbie sit drinking. Begbie is still keeping
a firm hand on the sports bag, which now holds the money.*

SICK BOY

So what are you planning with your share, Spud?

RENTON

Buy yourself that island in the sun?

99

For four fucking grand? One palm tree, a couple of rocks and a sewage outflow.

I don't know, maybe I'll buy something for my ma, and then buy some good speed, no bicarb like, then get a girl, take her out like, and treat her – properly.

Shag her senseless.

No, I don't mean like that – I mean something nice, like, that's all –

You daft cunt. If you're going to waste it like that, you might as well leave it all to me. Now get the drinks in.

I got a round already.

I got the last one.

It's your round, Franco.

Begbie stands up.

OK. Same again?

I'm off for a pish. When I come back, that money's still here, OK?

The moment you turn your back, we're out that door.

Sick Boy walks away towards the toilet.

I'll be right after you.

BEGBIE

You'll never catch us, you flabby bastard. Right, see, when I come
back –

RENTON

We'll be half-way down the road with the money.

BEGBIE

I'd fucking kill you.

RENTON

I guess you would, Franco.

Begbie walks away to the bar.

Spud and Renton look at each other and the bag of money.

Are you game for it?

*Spud looks at the bag and around the pub towards the toilet door and
Begbie.*

Begbie stands at the bar, awaiting the pints.

Well?

SPUD

Are you serious?

Renton looks around.

RENTON

I don't know. What do you think?

Spud says nothing. Suddenly they are interrupted.

SICK BOY

Still here, I see.

Sick Boy sits down.

RENTON

Yes, well, we wouldn't run out on a mate.

SICK BOY

Why not? I know I would. Where's Franco?

Renton turns to see Begbie making his way through the crowd with the pints held precariously.

As he reaches the table a Man standing with a group of friends accidentally nudges Begbie, causing a pint to spill over him.

BEGBIE

For fuck's sake.

MAN

Sorry, mate, I'll get you another.

BEGBIE

All down my fucking front, you fucking idiot.

MAN

Look, I'm sorry, I didn't mean it.

BEGBIE

Sorry's no going to dry me off, you cunt.

RENTON

Cool down, Franco. The guy's sorry.

BEGBIE

Not sorry enough for being a fat cunt.

MAN

Fuck you. If you can't hold a pint, you shouldn't be in the pub, mate. Now fuck off.

Begbie drops the remaining three pints.

As the Man looks down to the falling glasses, Begbie punches him in the face and knees him in the groin.

A fight breaks out between the Man and Begbie.

Sick Boy rushes forward to restrain Begbie.

Renton sits still, not even looking at the fight or what follows. His eyes are fixed on the bag while his hands fiddle.

Begbie stabs Spud in the hand.

Jesus Christ.

Good one, Franco.

BEGBIE

Shut your mouth or you'll be next.

SPUD

You've stabbed me, man.

BEGBIE

You were in my way.

Begbie, blade still in hand, addresses the entire pub.

And anyone in my way gets it, fucking gets it. Everybody hear that? Everybody happy?

Nobody says anything.

Renton is seated as before, avoiding Begbie's gaze.

Begbie addresses him.

Hey, Rent-boy, bring us down a smoke.

Renton does not move.

SICK BOY

We'd better go, Franco.

SPUD

I've got to get to the hospital, man.

BEGBIE
(to Spud)

You're not going to any fucking hospital.

(to Sick Boy)

You're staying there.

(to Renton)

And you bring me a fucking cigarette.

Renton swivels and stands up.

103

And the bag.

Renton lifts the bag and slowly approaches Begbie.

Renton, nervous, hand shaking, pulls a packet of cigarettes from a pocket and holds it towards Begbie.

Begbie does not move.

Renton holds out the bag.

Begbie takes it.

Now Renton selects a cigarette, puts it in his own lips and finds a lighter in another pocket.

He lights the cigarette and hands it over to Begbie.

Begbie inhales deeply and then blows the smoke towards Renton.

INT. HOTEL ROOM. DAY

Renton lies awake, sharing a bed with Sick Boy, who is asleep.

Spud and Begbie lie on the other, both asleep.

Begbie has an arm draped over the bag, holding it close.

Renton gets up and goes through to the small bathroom.

He puts the light on above the mirror and looks at himself. He washes his face and drinks a glass of water, then walks back to the bedroom.

Renton pulls on his jacket and shoes.

He stands over Begbie, then reaches carefully down to lift Begbie's arm up.

As he does so he realizes that Spud is watching him.

They say nothing.

Renton takes the bag.

Begbie stirs but does not wake.

[Renton looks down at Spud for a moment before unzipping the bag. He pulls out a small wad of cash, which he hands to Spud.

*Cut from completed film.

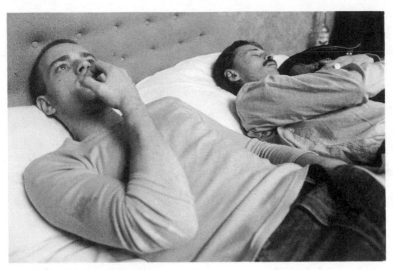

Spud tucks the wad away.]

Renton walks to the door and opens it.

He nods to Spud, then disappears.

INT. LOCKER. DAY

Envelope being removed.

INT. LEFT LUGGAGE. DAY

Renton takes the passport from the envelope.

EXT. STREET. DAY

Renton walks away.

> RENTON
> (*voice-over*)

Now, I've justified this to myself in all sorts of ways: it wasn't a big deal, just a minor betrayal, or we'd outgrown each other, you know, that sort of thing, but let's face it, I ripped them off. My so-called mates. But Begbie, I couldn't give a shit about him, and Sick Boy, well, he'd have done the same to me if only he'd thought of it first, and Spud, well, OK, I felt sorry for Spud – he never hurt anybody.

INT. HOTEL. DAY

Prostitutes, punters, Sick Boy and Spud line the corridor as two Policemen walk past towards:

INT. HOTEL ROOM. DAY

Begbie goes radge.

EXT. STREET. DAY

Renton continues his departure.

RENTON
(*voice-over*)

So why did I do it? I could offer a million answers, all false. The truth is that I'm a bad person, but that's going to change, I'm going to change. This is the last of this sort of thing. I'm cleaning up and I'm moving on, going straight and choosing life. I'm looking forward to it already. I'm going to be just like you: the job, the family, the fucking big television, the washing machine, the car, the compact disc and electrical tin opener, good health, low cholesterol, dental insurance, mortgage, starter home, leisurewear, luggage, three-piece suite, DIY, game shows, junk food, children, walks in the park, nine to five, good at golf, washing the car, choice of sweaters, family Christmas, indexed pension, tax exemption, clearing the gutters, getting by, looking ahead, to the day you die.

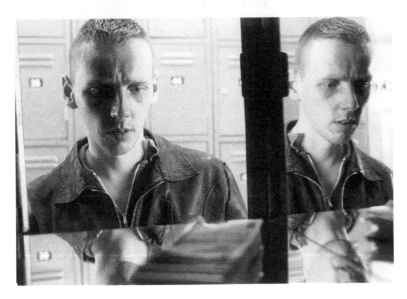

Miramax Films
Presents
TRAINSPOTTING

CAST

RENTON	Ewan McGregor
SPUD	Ewen Bremner
SICK BOY	Jonny Lee Miller
TOMMY	Kevin McKidd
BEGBIE	Robert Carlyle
DIANE	Kelly Macdonald
SWANNEY	Peter Mullan
MR RENTON	James Cosmo
MRS RENTON	Eileen Nicholas
ALLISON	Susan Vilder
LIZZY	Pauline Lynch
GAIL	Shirley Henderson
GAVIN (AND US TOURIST)	Stuart McQuarrie
MIKEY	Irvine Welsh
GAME SHOW HOST	Dale Winton
DEALER	Keith Allen
ANDREAS	Kevin Allen
GAIL'S MOTHER	Annie Louise Ross
GAIL'S FATHER	Billy Riddoch
DIANE'S MOTHER	Fiona Bell
DIANE'S FATHER	Vincent Friel
MAN I	Hugh Ross
MAN 2	Victor Eadie
WOMAN	Kate Donnelly
SHERIFF	Finlay Welsh
ESTATE AGENT	Eddie Nestor

CREW

Director	Danny Boyle
Producer	Andrew Macdonald
Screenplay	John Hodge
Director of Photography	Brian Tufano
Editor	Masahiro Hirakubo
Production Designer	Kave Quinn
Costume Designer	Rachel Fleming

Production Manager	Lesley Stewart
Casting	Gail Stevens
	Andy Pryor
Make-up Design	Graham Johnston
Art Director	Tracey Gallacher
First Assistant Director	David Gilchrist
Special Visual Effects	Grant Mason
	Tony Steers
Sound Recordist	Colin Nicolson
Second Assistant Director	Claire Hughes
Third Assistant Director	Ben Johnson
Script Supervisor	Anne Coulter
Floor Runners	Aidan Quinn
	Michael Queen
Production Accountant	Jennifer Booth
Production Coordinator	Shellie Smith
Assistant to the Producer	Jill Robertson
Production Runner	Kirstin McDougall
Location Manager	Robert How
Location Assistant	Saul Metzstein
Construction Manager	Colin H. Fraser
Set Dresser	Penny Crawford
Scenic Artist	Stuart Clarke
Draughtspersons	Jean Kerr
	Frances Connell
Assistant Art Director	Niki Longmuir
Art Department Assistants	Irene Harris
	Lorna J. Stewart
Art Department Runners	Miguel Rosenberg-Sapochnik
	Alan Payne
Art Department Trainee	Stephen Wong
Focus Puller	Robert Shipsey
Clapper Loader	Lewis Buchan
Grip	Adrian McCarthy
Steadicam Operator	Simon Bray
Camera Trainee	Neil Davidson
Boom Operator	Tony Cook
Sound Maintenance Engineer	Noel Thompson
Assembly Editor	Anuree de Silva
Assistant Editors	Neil Williams
	Denton Brown
FT2 Editing Trainee	Rab Wilson

Re-Recording Mixers	Brian Saunders
	Ray Merrin
	Mark Taylor
Effects Editor	Jonathan Miller
Dialogue Editor	Richard Fettes
Footsteps Editor	Martin Cantwell
Prop Master	Gordon Fitzgerald
Dressing Props	Piero Jamieson
	Mat Bergel
Standby Props	Stewart Cunningham
	Scott Keery
Construction Chargehand	Derek Fraser
Standby Carpenter	Bert Ross
Standby Stagehand	Brian Boyne
Carpenters	Brian Adams
	Richard Hassall
	Peter Knotts
	John Watt
Painters	James Patrick
	Paul Curren
	Bobby Gee
Stagehand	John Donnelly
Plasterer	Paterson Lindsay
Props Driver	Gregor Telfer
Props Trainees	Paul McNamara
	Michelle Bowker
Underwater Cameraman	Mike Valentine
Underwater Camera Assistant	Jim Kerr
Make-up and Hair	Robert McCann
Wardrobe Supervisor	Stephen Noble
Gaffer	Willie Cadden
Best Boy	Mark Ritchie
Electricians	Mark Ritchie
	Jimmy Dorigan
Genny Operator	John Duncan
Stills Photography	Liam Longman
Stunt Arranger	Terry Forrestal
Stunt Performers	Tom Delmar
	Nrinder Dhudwar
	Richard Hammatt
	Paul Heasman
	Tom Lucy

	Andreas Petrides
Special Technical Adviser	Eamon Doherty
Location Manager – London	Andrew Bainbridge
Location Assistant – London	Charlies Hiscott
London Contact	Lene Bausager
Action Vehicles	Robbie Ryan
Tracking Vehicles	Bikers of Coddenham Ltd
Facility Vehicles and Drivers	Bristol Television Film Services Ltd
Animal Handler	David Stewart
Camera Car Driver	Eric Smith
Caterers	Guy Cowan
	Fiona Cowan
	Allan Bell
	Jackie Douglas
	Isabel Graham
	Andy Irvine
	John McVeigh
Security	Dennis McFadden
	William Adams
	James Dunsmuir
	William Mackinnon
	Ian Miller
Completion Bond	Film Finances Ltd
Production Solicitors	Jonathan Berger
	Mishcon de Reya
Insurance	Sampson & Allen
Titles Design	Tomato
Opticals	Cine Image
Colour by	Rank Film Laboratories
Post Production Sound	The Sound Design Co.
Editing Facilities	Salon
Caterers	Reel Food
Arriflex camera and Zeiss lenses supplied by	Media Film Service London
Additional Camera Equipment	ICE
Lighting Equipment	Lee Lighting (Scotland) Ltd
Video Transfers	Midnight Transfer
Publicity	McDonald & Rutter
Originated on	Eastman Colour Film from Kodak
Freight	Ecosse World Express
Fido Services by	Cinesite Digital Film Center

Sound re-recorded at Delta Sound Services

Thanks to David Aukin, Allon Reich, Sara Geater, Carol Anne Docherty, Archie Macpherson, Jonathan Channon, Nicole Jacob, Kay Sheridan, Richard Findlay at Tods Murray WS.
Special thanks to David Bryce, Eamon Doherty and all at Calton Athletic Recovery Group for their inspiration and courage.

SOUNDTRACK AVAILABLE ON EMI RECORDS

'Lust for Life'
Words and music by Iggy Pop/David Bowie
Performed by Iggy Pop
Published by EMI Music Publishing Ltd/EMI Virgin Music Ltd/
Tintoretto Music administered by RZO Music
Courtesy of Virgin Records American Inc.

'Carmen – Habañera'
Composed by Georges Bizet
Courtesy of Laserlight/KPM

'Deep Blue Day'
Written by Brian Eno/Daniel Lanois/Roger Eno
Performed by Brian Eno
Published by Opal Music/Upala Music Inc./BMI
Courtesy of Virgin Records Ltd

'Trainspotting'
Words and music by Bobby Gillespie/Andrew Innes/Robert Young/
Martin Duffy
Performed by Primal Scream
Published by EMI Music Publishing Ltd/Complete Music Ltd
Courtesy of Creation Records Ltd

'Temptation'
Words and music by Ian Marsh/Martyn Ware/Glen Gregory
Performed by Heaven 17
Published by EMI Virgin Music Ltd/Sound Diagrams Ltd/Warner
Chappell Music Ltd
Courtesy of Virgin Records Ltd

'Atomic'
Written by Deborah Harry/Jimmy Destri
Performed by Sleeper
Published by Chrysalis Music Inc/Monster Island Music (Ascap)
Courtesy of Indolent Records/BMG Records (UK) Ltd

'Temptation'
Written by Stephen Morris/Peter Hook/Bernard Sumner/Gillian Gilbert
Performed by New Order
Published by Be Music//Warner Chappell Music Ltd
Courtesy of London Records Ltd (UK)

'Nightclubbing'
Words and music by Iggy Pop/David Bowie
Performed by Iggy Pop
Published by EMI Music Publishing Ltd/EMI Virgin Music Ltd/
Tintoretto Music administered by RZO Music
Courtesy of Virgin Records America Inc

'Sing'
Lyrics by Damon Albarn
Music by Damon Albarn/Graham Coxon/Alex James/David Rowntree
Performed by Blur
Published by MCA Music Ltd
Licensed by EMI Records Ltd by courtesy of Parlophone
and EMI Special Markets UK

'Perfect Day'
Words and music by Lou Reed
Performed by Lou Reed
Published by Screen Gems-EMI Music Ltd
Courtesy of BMG UK Ltd on behalf of BMG Music

'Dark and Long (Dark Train Mix)'
Words and music by Rick Smith/Karl Hyde/Darren Emerson
Performed by Underworld
Published by Sherlock Holmes Music Ltd
Courtesy of Junior Boy's Own, London

'Think About the Way (Born Digi Digi Bom . . .)'
Written by Roberto Zanetti
Performed by Ice MC
Published by Extravaganza Publishing/Artemis BV
By kind permission of Warner Chappell Music Ltd
Courtesy of Robyx SRL/Warner Music UK Ltd

113

'Mile End'
Written by Banks/Cocker/Doyle/Mackey/Senior/Webber
Performed by Pulp
Published by Island Music Ltd
Courtesy of Island Records Ltd

'For What You Dream of (Full on Renaissance Mix)'
Written by John Digweed/Nick Muir/Carol Leeming
Performed by Bedrock featuring Kyo
Published by Seven PM Music/Sony Music Publishing/
Peermusic (UK) Ltd
Courtesy of Stress Recordings

'2.1'
Written by Donna Lorraine Matthews
Performed by Elastica
Published by EMI Music Publishing Ltd
Courtesy of DGC Records and Deceptive Records Ltd

'Hertzlich tut mich verlangen'
Composed by J S Bach
Performed by Gabor Lehotka
Courtesy of Laserlight/KPM

'Two Little Boys'
Words and music by Edward Madden/Theodore Morse
Performed by Ewen Bremner
Published by Herman Darewski Music Publishing Co/EMI Publishing Ltd/
Redwood Music Ltd (Carlin)

'A Final Hit'
Written by Neil Barnes/Paul Daley
Performed by Leftfield
Published by Hard (UK) Hands Publishing Ltd/Chrysalis Music Ltd
Courtesy of Hard Hands/Columbia Records
by arrangement with Sony Music Entertainment (UK) Ltd

'Statuesque'
Song and words by Wener
Music by Wener, Stewart, Maclure, Osman
Performed by Sleeper
Published by Sony Music Publishing
Courtesy of Indolent Records/BMG Records (UK) Ltd

'Born Slippy (Nuxx)'
Words and music by Rick Smith/Karl Hyde
Performed by Underworld
Published by Sherlock Holmes Music Ltd
Courtesy of Junior Boy's Own, London

'Closet Romantic'
Written by Damon Albarn
Performed by Albarn, Gauld, Sidwell, Henry, Smith
and The Duke Strings Quartet
Published by MCA Music Ltd
Licensed by EMI Records Ltd by courtesy of Parlophone and EMI
Special Markets UK

Television Clips
Archie Gemmill goal
Courtesy of Worldmark
Horseracing
Courtesy of International Racecourse Management Ltd

Filmed on location in Glasgow, Edinburgh and London

The story, all names, characters and incidents portrayed in this
production are fictitious. No identification with actual persons, places,
buildings and products is intended or should be inferred.

A Figment Film in association with Noel Gay Motion Picture
Company Ltd
for Channel Four

© Channel Four Television Corporation
MCMXCV

AFTERWORD

Danny Boyle with Irvine Welsh

AFTERWORD –
INTERVIEW WITH IRVINE WELSH

This interview with Irvine Welsh was conducted during the film's penultimate week of shooting. Welsh had flown over especially from Amsterdam, where he now lives, to do a cameo performance as the drug dealer Mikey Forrester.

KEVIN MACDONALD: *Did you ever consider when you were writing the book, or when it was published, that it might be turned into a film?*
IRVINE WELSH: I never even considered that the book would be published in the first place – I never thought about it in terms of publication – so getting it published was a big enough surprise, it being successful was a surprise and then it being made into a play was a surprise and now it being made into a film is a surprise. So it's just been a series of different surprises that I've become quite inured to. I don't see what can possibly happen to it next. Surely this has to be the end!

KM: *When Andrew, Danny and John got in touch with you and said they were interested in doing the film, what was your immediate response?*

IW: I thought it was quite brave of them to do because, especially with the success of *Shallow Grave*, they could have taken big bucks in Hollywood. I couldn't really see it as a film at first just because of it being episodic and not a strong kind of narrative thing. But on the other hand, I couldn't see it as a play before it became a successful play, so it's got an appeal. I think that a lot of people are sick of the kind of representations of the world that we live in as a kind of bland *Four Weddings and a Funeral* sort of place – they want something that says a wee bit more about the society that we actually live in and a wee bit more about the different cultures within that society that tend to be ignored.

KM: *Do you think that the film will be faithful to your book?*
IW: I think that as an author the first thing you have to tell yourself is: I wrote the book but somebody else is making the film. The whole point of it – the exciting part of it – is that it's going to be transformed in some way. The more transformation the better from my point of view. People go on about a 'faithful interpretation', but you can't have a faithful interpretation of something; you can maybe have it in spirit, but it's going to change as it moves into a different medium. I think that with film or any other different medium, you don't have the same degree of freedom as you maybe do with the blank page, on to which you can put whatever you like. You can build up a lot of psychological depth to the characters in a book, whereas in film you've really got to take a line on it and say, maybe, is this a black comedy or is this social realism? And then stick to that line. Anyway, that's the exciting part about it: how people are going to see it, how they're going to interpret it. It is open to so many different interpretations, and it's something that I change my own mind about quite a lot.

KM: *Are you glad that they haven't taken the social realist approach?*
IW: Yes, I am kind of happy with that. I think I would have been a wee bit despondent if – not to knock Ken Loach or anything because I think that he's brilliant at what he does – if they had made it in the Loach fashion because I don't think we need another Ken Loach. I would have been disappointed if it had been a kind of worthy piece of social realism. I think there's more to it than that. It's about the culture and the lifestyle in a non-

judgemental way. It's about how people live their lives and how people interact. To see it as just a kind of reaction to social oppression, to social circumstances, is to rip some of the soul out of it and to make the characters into victims. I don't think that they really are. I think that they're people whose ideals and ambitions perhaps outstrip what society has to offer them, but I think they've got great strength in spite of that.

KM: *How did you find performing in the film?*
IW: You admire the discipline that actors have. I've now worked a fair bit with actors over the year and I used to think of it as very much a bunch of people poncing around on stage. But the effort, the concentration and work that goes into it from the actors and the whole crew . . . you see really what a sweaty, grafting kind of work-intensive industry it is. It destroys my stereotype that I had about actors, theatre, film people, all of that, of being a bit kind of effeminate. The reality is very different.

KM: *Were you surprised when Danny asked you to do this little cameo?*
IW: I wasn't surprised in a sense. It's something that I would have done if I'd been him because its effective. It stops the author from criticizing the film because you can't say, 'Oh, my God, they've ruined my book!' because you've been a part of the whole process and you've joined in. That's a kind of frivolous thing to say, but I think that it always adds a bit of intrigue.

KM: *What part are you playing?*
IW: I'm playing this drugs dealer who's probably one of the least sympathetic characters in the book. He's a kind of pretty manipulative, nasty, horrible guy, so a lot of people will say type-casting again!

KM: *Do you think that* Trainspotting – *the book – is dated in any way?*
IW: Yes, it's dated in the context of Edinburgh because the whole drug scene has changed slightly there. It's still a 'Class A' drug society, but there's fewer people who are doing smack these days and who are into that hard-core subculture . . . it's being managed through methadone programmes. That use of heroin had moved through to Glasgow. Probably up until a couple of years ago *Trainspotting* was more applicable to Glasgow than it was to

Edinburgh. The thing had moved. But the drug which people chose to fuck up on isn't really the issue. The fact is that there's just so few opportunities for people that it's not surprising that they try to escape from it or try to obliterate as much of the pain of the world as possible. So while the drugs may have changed, the issues are just the same. People have always abused drugs. Traditionally it's been alcohol, now it's a cocktail of different drugs simply because there are different drugs available. It doesn't really matter whether it's heroin or alcohol or whatever. In fact, you're probably better off being a junkie than an alcoholic because if you're a junkie you can reform quite successfully if you just change the people that you're hanging around with. It's very difficult for an alcoholic to do that because you're being bombarded with these messages all the time about drinking and it's so much a part of the culture, whereas you can move out of the smack subculture.

KM: *So it's not a period piece?*
IW: No. If you're being pedantic about it, you could say that it was set in Edinburgh between 1982 and 1988, but the issues of drug addiction and drug abuse and the on-going HIV issues are as pertinent as ever – probably more so now.

KM: *What was your opinion of* Shallow Grave *– and did you think the makers of that film had the right abilities or vision for a film of* Trainspotting?
IW: Yes. I only saw *Shallow Grave* a couple of days ago on video – it's just been a series of coincidences that I didn't see it when I was in Britain, and then I moved to Holland and then when it came to Holland it was only there for a day before I was off to the States. But I have seen a video of it. What appealed to me about *Shallow Grave* was the constant action and movement. I think that sits really well with the bias towards action that modern writing has, that constant motion and movement, keeping things moving and keeping things happening – the kind of visceral, hard-edged humour sits well. The characterizations and characters were completely different and I didn't find the characters particularly empathetic – I couldn't particularly care for the characters – but maybe that's just where I'm coming from. That might just be a class or cultural thing. Everybody I know seemed to feel really sort

of gleeful when Ewan [McGregor] got punched and then got his legs broken! But the other thing I liked about it was the sheer beauty of the camerawork and the use of colours – primary colours. That detail in film-making and that kind of craft and stylization have really been absent in British films, and that was one of the things that really appealed to me.

John Hodge wrote the screenplay for *Shallow Grave*. A doctor by trade, he has now focused his attention almost entirely on writing. Born in Glasgow, he now lives in Edinburgh.